Friendship
Evangelism
By The **Book**

Applying First Century Principles to Twenty-First Century Relationships

●

TOM STEBBINS

CHRISTIAN PUBLICATIONS
Camp Hill, Pennsylvania

Christian Publications
3825 Hartzdale Drive, Camp Hill, PA 17011

Faithful, biblical publishing since 1883

ISBN: 0-87509-584-4
LOC Catalog Card Number: 94-69037
© 1995 by Christian Publications
All rights reserved
Printed in the United States of America

95 96 97 98 99   5   4   3   2

Cover design by Linda Wood

Contents

91172

Foreword

WHEN TOM STEBBINS writes anything about evangelism, he writes as a certified expert in the field. Having spent many years as a pastor, foreign missionary, evangelist, seminary professor, as well as clinic teacher and instructor for Evangelism Explosion International, he is thoroughly familiar with the field. He practices what he preaches and writes from no ivory tower.

Most so-called friendship evangelism programs have about 99 percent friendship and one percent evangelism; in fact, many of them are 100 percent friendship and zero percent evangelism. This is not the case, however, with the friendship evangelism set forth by Tom Stebbins. He knows full well that without the evangel, there is no evangelism—that unless the content of the gospel is conveyed, it is deceit and fraud to call a program evangelism of any kind.

Here you will find practical, biblically based methods of making friends, establishing rapport, gaining confidence and moving graciously to the gospel. We at Evangelism Explosion are so impressed with this work that we are going to use it as an advanced course in our train-ing.

May God multiply its effects exponentially.

D. James Kennedy, Ph.D.
President and Founder
Evangelism Explosion
International

Preface

FRIENDSHIP EVANGELISM, in recent years, has moved to center stage in the evangelical world's endeavors to reach lost people for Christ.

For some people friendship evangelism means developing meaningful, loving relationships with unchurched people so that in God's time and way they may be attracted to Jesus.

To others, the term stands for "living the life" and "sharing the love of Jesus" with neighbors, fellow employees, personal acquaintances, sports buddies and the extended family.

Then there are those who see it as inviting friends to their home for dinner, a cookout or a Bible study in hopes of creating an opportunity to share with them the good news of Jesus.

Increasing numbers of churches view it as special "Friendship Sundays" when well-known Christian musicians, businessmen, athletes or politicians share their testimony. Church members are encouraged to bring their friends to hear the gospel as it is presented in song or word.

Joseph Aldrich, author of *Friendship Evangelism* and *Gentle Persuasion*, describes friendship evangelism as "loving people until they ask why." Rebecca Manley Pippert, in her book *Out of the Saltshaker*, suggests that it is getting the church out of the sanctuary and into the world. D. James Kennedy, author of *Evangelism Explosion*, calls it witnessing as a way of life. Jim Peterson in *Living Proof* writes about it in terms of engaging people "on their own turf." All of these books are outstanding! Their authors have given us invaluable, practical insights on the subject.

But, in all of my reading, I have yet to discover a book approaching friendship evangelism from a totally biblical perspective. By that I mean (1) starting with a study of the Scriptures, (2) discovering what they say about friendship evangelism and then (3) applying those biblical principles to an every-member, churchwide friendship evangelism strategy.

That's the approach I've taken in this book. That's why, as you probably have already guessed, I have entitled it *Friendship Evangelism by the Book*. In the past three years as I have studied God's Word chapter by chapter, two questions have been in the back of my mind: *How did Jesus and the early Christians evangelize? How can I apply first-century principles of evangelism to my contemporary relationships?* The 13 chapters of this book are my answer to that question.

At heart I'm basically a storyteller. As a child I loved the bedtime stories my older sister,

Hariette, told me. My favorite preachers were those whose sermons were sprinkled with anecdotes. In fact, I came to Christ under the preaching of one of the greatest storytellers I've ever met: Merv Roselle. Thus you will find a liberal number of stories—true, real life stories—throughout the book.

Jesus' supreme purpose in coming into the world was to redeem the world for God. Everything He did was motivated by that purpose. If we, therefore, desire to reach the world for Christ, we need to research carefully *how* Jesus fulfilled that motivating purpose. As we examine how He and His first followers evangelized, we will see that it was through relationships, through friendships.

Another factor contributed to this writing project. I serve as associate pastor for outreach at Christ Community Church (The Christian and Missionary Alliance) in Omaha, Nebraska. Our board of elders engaged the services of Dr. James F. Engel, author of *What's Gone Wrong with the Harvest?* and an outstanding communications and church growth authority.

Engel led us through a very thorough congregational survey. After analyzing the results, he reported that our church was in a strategic location and had great potential to build bridges to the unchurched and attract them to Christ. "But," he added, "you aren't doing a very good job of reaching the unchurched."

This observation greatly surprised me. At the

time, we had certified over a thousand of our people in Evangelism Explosion! Engel shocked me further by saying that most of our members confined their social life within the church. They didn't know their neighbors very well; most of them saw themselves as inadequately prepared for effective witness to nonchristians.

To address this situation, Engel suggested that, as soon as possible, our church initiate friendship evangelism training. And because of the high percentage of adults in adult Sunday school, he recommended that we do our training there.

I knew our adults would not appreciate the substitution of evangelism training for their weekly lesson in the Word. But I also knew that they didn't much enjoy the review lesson that came at the end of every quarter. So I asked permission to substitute a lesson on biblical evangelism for the quarterly review lesson.

The chapters of this book are, in effect, 13 of those friendship evangelism Bible expositions. Over the past more than three years we used them to motivate and mobilize our congregation. By offering a new lesson each quarter, we have been able to give our people new biblical insights and fresh reminders to continue friendship evangelism as an everyday lifestyle. In fact, I continue to prepare a new lesson every quarter. Because it is so vital to the outreach mind-set of our people, I shall continue to do so.

Christian Publications, Inc., published my first four lessons in a notebook, complete with overhead transparencies and student notes entitled *Oikos Outreach 4 Times a Year*. That made it possible for other churches—small and large—to use these lessons in their adult Sunday school classes and equip their people for reaching out to their friends. Some pastors have adapted the lessons into Sunday morning messages to create a friendship evangelism mind-set in their congregations. With the publication of this book, those churches will be able to continue their training. I anticipate further that this book will be used as a text for advanced level training in Evangelism Explosion.

Speaking of Evangelism Explosion (EE), I want you to know I am a strong advocate of EE! In 1977, EE gave me a very biblical strategy to use in my pastorate at Kowloon Tong Alliance Church in Hong Kong. It enabled me to mobilize and equip members of our international congregation for personal evangelism. In three years we saw the church grow from 60 people to 350!

Since moving to Omaha in 1980, I have continued to equip lay people through EE. This strategy has contributed to the growth of our church here as well. We have seen our Sunday morning attendance triple!

But, as I mentioned earlier, many members of our congregation were not touched by our EE training. Either they felt they were too advanced in years to do the memory work or too involved in other ministries to enlist in the training.

I'm happy to report that our friendship evangelism training did not compete with the EE ministry. Rather, it complemented it! It has involved many people who for one reason or another were not able to take EE training. And, it has given to our EE-trained people a new sensitivity for, and greater vision to reach, their friends, relatives, associates and neighbors for Christ.

Repeat: Evangelism Explosion and friendship evangelism have complemented each other beautifully! By studying these lessons, our EE-trained people have refined their relational skills and learned how to maximize their network of trust relationships for sharing the gospel. And many of our people, while reaching out to their friends, have discovered that they are unprepared to effectively present the gospel and have since enrolled in EE.

Jan, for instance, is a busy housewife whose children have grown up and "left the nest." Five days a week she helps her husband, Kent, in their insurance business. Once a week, during good weather, she participates in a women's golf league. On Sundays and occasionally on week nights she serves in various church ministries.

Several years ago Jan enrolled in EE. In the

ensuing years she and her team have seen a number of people come to Christ. But that fruit was outside her natural network of relationships.

Then three years ago Jan's Sunday school class started studying our quarterly Bible lessons on evangelism. Jan's concern for the women in her golf league increased. When one of her friends in the league was hospitalized with cancer, Jan began visiting her regularly, expressing the love of Christ. One joyous day God opened the door for Jan to share the good news about Jesus, and her friend prayed to invite the Savior into her life!

Jan's husband, Kent, in order to serve as a church elder, was required to take EE training. Not normally an aggressive conversationalist, Kent found that EE equipped him to open conversations easily and to lead naturally into the gospel. One day, after selling a woman an insurance policy, he pushed back his chair.

"Ma'am," he said calmly, "when you die, this policy will take care of your family. But it won't do anything to help you." Taken aback by his comment, the woman asked what he meant. So Kent asked permission to share with her EE's two diagnostic questions.

"If you were to die today," Kent began, "do you know for certain that you would go to be with God in heaven?" His client wasn't sure, so he asked her the second question: "Suppose you were to die and stand before God and He asked you, 'Why should I let you into My heaven?' What would you reply?"

The woman was open for Kent to share the gospel. Concluding his simple presentation, Kent joyfully helped her pray to invite Christ into her life as Savior and Lord!

Friendship evangelism training aided Jan to lovingly share the gospel with her golf friend. Evangelism Explosion training equipped Kent to lead a customer to Christ! This book can motivate and equip you to reach your friends for Christ.

I sincerely pray that you will be helped by our adventure together through the following 13 chapters. Right now I invite you to turn to chapter one for some exciting biblical insights into the vital subject of being a true friend.

Thomas H. Stebbins
Omaha, Nebraska
August, 1994

Being a True Friend

Mark 2:1-12

TWO FRIENDS WERE driving my wife, Donna, and me from St. Petersburg, Florida, to Fort Lauderdale. As we cruised down Interstate 75 right at the speed limit, I was reasonably certain we would arrive on time for the important meeting I was to attend.

Suddenly, the station wagon began to lose speed and finally sputtered to a stop. My heart almost stopped with it. How would I get to Fort Lauderdale on time? Fortunately, we were within sight of the next exit. Donna and I offered to walk to the exit for help. We were about halfway there when two middle-aged men in a pickup pulled over.

"Oh, excuse us!" one of them explained. "We

thought you were friends of ours because your car is just like theirs!" Then he added, "Why don't you jump in and be our friends anyhow?" We crowded into the cab and our newfound friends dropped us off at the nearest gas station, where I called an AAA wrecker for a tow. Then I tried to phone for a rental car that I could drive to Fort Lauderdale for my meeting.

I discovered there were no rental cars in that small town. But a young man in the next phone booth overheard my conversation. "My name is Tom," he volunteered. "I'm driving to Fort Myers. Why don't you ride with me? I'll drop you off at the airport there, where I'm sure you can rent a car." Tom first took us back to our friends in the station wagon to pick up our suitcases and explain our plans. And in short order we were on our way. Though a bit late, I was able to make my meeting!

As I've thought back over the chaotic events of that day, the helpfulness of those friends—both long-term and new—stands out above all else. Indeed, the friend in time of need is priceless!

A friend has been variously defined. "A person who knows all about you and loves you anyway." "One who never gets in the way except when you are on the way down" "One who steps in when the whole world steps out."

Solomon said, "A friend loves at all times,

and a brother is born for adversity." (Proverbs 17:17). Jesus said, "Greater love has no one than this, that he lay down his life for his friends" (John 15:13).

Today more and more people are becoming excited about reaching their friends for Christ. That's healthy! But not everyone understands what is involved in becoming the true friend so essential to friendship evangelism. As we begin to consider friendship evangelism by the Book, we must first understand what true, biblical, friendship is. Some will jump on the bandwagon, become a little nicer to their friends, invite them occasionally to church and assume that they're doing friendship evangelism. That's good, but not good enough!

So exactly what do we mean by that word *friend*, and how do we become one?

There is no person more lonely and despondent than the one who needs a true friend but has none! Such a person was the invalid who lay by the Bethesda Pool for 38 years (John 5:1-9). When Jesus saw him lying there and learned he had been in that condition that long, He asked the man if he wanted to get well.

"Sir," replied the man, "I have no one to help me into the pool when the water is stirred" (John 5:7). For 38 years he was without one friend to help. How sad! Thank God for Jesus who came along in the man's time of need and befriended him.

We've all heard about Job's friends. But what did Job himself say about those friends? "A despairing man should have the devotion of his friends, . . . But my brothers are as undependable as intermittent streams" (Job 6:14-15).

David, too, was greatly disappointed by his friends who failed him when he needed them most:

> My heart pounds, my strength fails
> me;
> even the light has gone from my
> eyes.
> My friends and companions avoid me
> because of my wounds;
> my neighbors stay far away.
> (Psalm 38:10-11)

In contrast to the Bethesda paralytic and Job and David, there was a man who happily found some true friends who stepped in to help him at his moment of great need. Like the man at the Bethesda Pool, he was an invalid. Here's the miracle as Mark describes it:

> A few days later, when Jesus again entered Capernaum, the people heard that he had come home. So many gathered that there was no room left, not even outside the door, and he preached the word to them. Some men came, bringing to him a

paralytic, carried by four of them. Since they could not get him to Jesus because of the crowd, they made an opening in the roof above Jesus and, after digging through it, lowered the mat the paralyzed man was lying on. When Jesus saw their faith, he said to the paralytic, "Son, your sins are forgiven."

Now some teachers of the law were sitting there, thinking to themselves, "Why does this fellow talk like that? He's blaspheming! Who can forgive sins but God alone?"

Immediately Jesus knew in his spirit that this was what they were thinking in their hearts, and he said to them, "Why are you thinking these things? Which is easier: to say to the paralytic, 'Your sins are forgiven,' or to say, 'Get up, take your mat and walk'? But that you may know that the Son of Man has authority on earth to forgive sins . . . ." He said to the paralytic, "I tell you, get up, take your mat and go home." He got up, took his mat and walked out in full view of them all. This amazed everyone and they praised God, saying, "We have never seen anything like this!" (Mark 2:1-12).

What is the main lesson from this episode in Jesus' life? It is this: *A true friend helps at the moment of greatest need; the other's greatest need is Jesus Christ.* Isn't that what friendship evangelism is all about?

How then would you describe in detail a "friendship evangelist?" From this account in Mark 2 let me suggest five adjectives that describe such a person. First, he must be . . .

1. Compassionate

The four men in this narrative were compassionate friends. Convinced that Jesus could heal their paralyzed friend, they presumably left the crowded house where Jesus was preaching and went to their needy friend. Then they did something extremely helpful: they brought the man to Jesus. To be compassionate, we too must . . .

a. Reach friends outside the church.

I see in the first part of the story the church of Jesus Christ in microcosm. Christ is central in the house. He is preaching the Word. People from the world have gathered around Him to marvel and to be taught. It is the church at worship. But as important as worship is, there is one more essential element: The church, to be the true church, must be the church in mission! How beautiful, then, to see Christ's followers outside the four walls of the "church" bringing their needy friend to Jesus!

The helpless invalid certainly is a picture of the sin-sick world—your lost friends, associates and neighbors who live and work in the community which surrounds your church. They're helpless in their sins and can do nothing to save themselves. They're hurting. They are in desperate need of your Savior-Healer.

The real question is: Will you compassionately reach out to your friends outside the walls of your church? It is important that you empathetically . . .

b. See your friends' needs.

Notice, in verse 6, that the scribes weren't aware of the paralyzed man's need. They were too busy criticizing Jesus' ministry. While they were reasoning in their cold, calloused hearts, the four compassionate followers of Jesus were reaching out to their hurting friend. These friends in need were friends indeed.

You and I need to remember that our friends' lives, like a pendulum, are constantly moving back and forth between times of crisis and times of calm, between responsiveness and resistance. Generally, our friends are much more responsive to our love and witness in their times of crisis. Therefore, like the four men in the story, we need to be alert and quick to . . .

c. Do something practical for them.

True compassion feels people's hurts and

reaches out to help in tangible ways. The four friends did something intensely practical. They did not simply tell the man where he could go for help; they themselves took him to Jesus. Someone has written:

> *Words* are easy, like the wind.
> Faithful friends are hard to find.
> He who is your friend indeed
> He will *help* you in your need.

The purpose of the church is not just to share words of truth within our places of worship but to demonstrate the love of Christ to the needy world outside our places of worship.

I heard of an 18-year-old who could not pass up an opportunity to steal. Finally he was caught and incarcerated. While in prison he found a Gideon Bible, read it and gave his heart to Christ. Upon his release from prison he found a job as a bank teller. On his second day at work, he was accosted by the bank manager, who had learned of the fellow's prison record.

"Would you mind telling me what you were put in jail for and what you're doing handling this bank's money?" The youth responded that he had been converted and wanted to put himself to the test.

"Suppose you fail the test," the manager replied. "If you want to stay at this job, you'll have to get me five bank certificates of $5,000 as security!"

Discouraged, the lad called his pastor, who got on the phone with several businessmen in his congregation. In a matter of hours he received 10 $5,000 certificates. Talk about compassion! Those businessmen did something practical! They were true friends!

A friendship evangelist also needs to be . . .

2. Creative

Notice that the four friends of the paralyzed man did something very creative to get their friend to Jesus. They lowered him through a hole they made in the roof!

Some people are more creative than others. But made in the image of our Creator, all of us have within us some creative juices if we'll but use them! Now if you are truly creative . . .

a. Don't take *no* for an answer.

The Bible says so many people were gathered in the house where Jesus was speaking that "there was no room left, not even outside the door." So when the four men brought their friend to Jesus, the crowd, no doubt, cried out, "No way! Impossible! You can't get in!"

But the four compassionate, determined men wouldn't be turned back from their saving, healing mission! They found a stairway on the outside of the house that led up to the flat roof. Then they dug a hole through the dirt-covered tiles and lowered their friend into Jesus' presence.

If necessity is the mother of invention, then the hurt of a friend should give birth to creativity!

A Christian doctor tried everything to share Christ with his friends, but he was constantly rebuffed. The doctor had a talent, however, that all of his friends appreciated. He could play the trumpet incredibly well. His friends were always asking him to play for them. So one day he came up with a very imaginative approach to sharing the gospel. He recorded a series of solos on a cassette dealing with topics such as heaven, man's sin, God's love, Christ's saving death on the cross and faith. Then, between each solo he wove his testimony, a gospel explanation, some Scripture and a few illustrations. His friends loved it! And he was able to sow the seed of God's Word in their hearts. He wouldn't take *no* for an answer. And this forced him to find a creative means for evangelism.

b. Do something no one else thought of.

Who would ever think of bringing a friend to Jesus through an opening in a roof? It was just the kind of bold, unstereotyped, innovative "breakthrough" that was needed to get the job done!

Isabel, of Pompano Beach, Florida, wanted to witness to her neighborhood and to the drug community nearby, but at her advanced age, she didn't have the strength to do it. After praying about the matter, she felt led to enroll in her local church's EE training program. Next, she bought an antique car and had it painted in bright colors. Then she purchased some beautiful early American dresses and bonnets.

When she had everything in place, she systematically and prayerfully drove her little eye-catching jalopy to carefully selected parking spots in her neighborhood and in the inner city. Everywhere she parked, friends, neighbors and scores of inner city youth came to ask about her vehicle and attire. It gave her golden opportunities to distribute literature, answer questions and share the gospel with people in a way that no one else had thought of!

c. Remember, some may say you're crazy!

Remember, too, something else: Some of the wisest people who have left the greatest impact on history were thought crazy—Christopher Columbus, Abraham Lincoln, John Wesley and the Wright brothers, just to name a few.

Jesus' contemporaries also questioned His sanity (Mark 3:21), and some people in Corinth evidently wondered about Paul (2 Corinthians 5:13).

The preaching of the cross is foolishness to those who perish. And if you're going to do something creative to bring your friends to Christ, you may have to risk being thought a little odd or "extreme."

Next, if you're going to become a true friendship evangelist, you will, like the four men who brought their friend to Christ, need to do something . . .

3. Costly

It may be accurately stated that while eternal life is free, it cost Jesus His life. And it will cost you a great deal to bring salvation to your lost friends, family members and neighbors. First you'll need to . . .

a. Devote some quality time to the task.

You, like the four men, will have to set aside time to become acquainted with your friends and neighbors so you'll understand their needs. You'll want to invest time praying for them, visiting with them, building bridges to them and becoming involved in activities which interest them. And you'll need to . . .

b. Invest some all-out effort.

The paralytic in Mark 2 was no light load. As clumsy as a paralyzed man lying on a cot might be, it must have taken quite an effort to carry him through the streets, up the steps onto the roof and then to open a hole in the roof and lower his cot into the room where Jesus was speaking.

You, too, will need to expend much effort to

bring your friends to Christ. There just isn't any easy way and there aren't any shortcuts to friendship evangelism.

Don, in Chatham, New Jersey, noticed that two of his neighbors had a difficult time keeping the snow off their driveways, so each winter he did the shoveling for them. When the church hosted a friendship banquet, he invited his two neighbors to join him. To his great surprise, both of them gave their hearts to Christ. Then, to follow them up he invested more effort discipling them.

Another costly step you'll want to consider is to . . .

c. Sacrifice some personal funds.

Though Mark doesn't allude to it, certainly when the miracle was complete and the meeting was coming to a close, one of the four men must have turned to the owner of the house and offered to fix the roof or at least pay for someone else to repair the damages. Clearly, it cost the four men financially to bring their friend to Jesus.

An EE team came back from calling on a church visitor and reported to the class that the person they had led to Christ needed a stove. Before the report session was over, two men volunteered to help: one to buy the person a stove and the other to deliver the stove in his pick-up truck.

The above team endeavor reminds us that the friendship evangelist's task is almost always . . .

4. Cooperative

Bringing the paralytic friend to Jesus was a team effort. Each of the four persons had to carry his part of the load. Likewise, if you are to be effective, you need to . . .

a. Involve others from within the church.

A visiting pastor once asked his fellow clergyman how many members he had in his church.

"You made three mistakes in your question," the other pastor replied. "First, it's not my church but Christ's. Second, it isn't a church; it's a mission. Third, we don't have members, we have ministers."

There's nothing more exciting than seeing a church become a mission in the true sense of the term, a congregation become a mighty army, pew sitters become active ministers, a community of worshipers become living, friendly witnesses!

If you're going to have such a team effort, you must . . .

b. Draw on others' gifts and talents.

Most of the teaching regarding the gifts of the Spirit today advises Christians to discover their gift or gifts. It exhorts them to bring edification *within* Christ's Body, the Church. More emphasis needs to be placed upon members of that Body also using their gifts to win lost people *outside* the four walls of their churches. Gifts of help, hospitality, mercy, benevolence, teaching and other gifts can and should be employed to enhance a loving outreach to friends, neighbors, relatives.

Thus you will . . .

c. Allow others to enter into your joy.

Mark, in his narrative, tells us that when the paralytic took up his bed and walked home, it "amazed everyone and they praised God, saying, 'We have never seen anything like this!' " (2:12).

There is no greater joy than seeing a friend come to Christ and seeing his or her physical and spiritual needs met. And when others share with you in the saving mission, your joy is multiplied.

In Dayton, Ohio, a house caught fire and burned to the ground. Before the flame was even extinguished, neighbors and friends from a local Alliance church came to the rescue. Some brought the bereaved family to their home for shelter. Others brought food. Still others contributed clothing and bedding. When the family who lost everything finally got back on their feet, they visited the congregation that had been so loving and helpful. And in the process of time they gave their hearts to Christ.

When you come right down to it, that's the important thing. Are you influencing your friends for Christ?

In the fifth place the friendship evangelist must be . . .

5. Christ-centered

Notice that throughout the narrative the focus is not upon the church, not on religion, but upon Christ! The scribes had religion, but it didn't do much for the paralytic. The four men brought their friend to Christ. So today you need to . . .

a. Let Christ heal your friends' hurts.

All around us are people with deep needs. They have physical, emotional, relational hurts. Their cares weigh them down almost to despair. And our Christ has the answer!

But even deeper, there is a spiritual need that is the real source of their difficulty. It is called sin: S-I-N. And Christ has the answer to that problem, too. So you need to . . .

b. Present Jesus as the One Who forgives.

The same Jesus Who said to the paralytic, "Take your mat and go home" also said, "Your sins are forgiven."

You live in a society where one of the greatest needs is for forgiveness. You have a message of forgiveness and a Savior Who offers that forgiveness. May you vigilantly watch for choice opportunities to introduce your friends to Jesus. And then . . .

c. Trust Jesus to give your friends lasting help.

Mark tells us that when Jesus saw *their* faith—that is, the joint faith of the four men—He wrought the miracle and granted forgiveness. Faith is always the important ingredient. You must trust Christ implicitly to meet your friends' needs and to bring them lasting help.

At 5 o'clock one morning Tom's phone rang and awoke him out of a deep sleep. It was Jerry, one of the customers whom Tom had befriended.

"I'm calling to say goodbye," Jerry said.

"I didn't know you were leaving us," Tom replied, still not fully awake. "Where are you going?"

"I'm going to end it all," Jerry explained. Suddenly Tom was wide awake.

"Wait, Jerry!" Tom pleaded. "I'll be there in 15 minutes!"

When Tom arrived at Jerry's house, Jerry explained that his wife had died of leukemia leaving hospital bills of a million dollars. Even after insurance, there were $400,000 due. From 5:30 in the morning until 1:00 in the afternoon Tom counseled his friend. At last Jerry gave his

heart to Christ, found the forgiveness and en-
couragement he needed and is today a growing
Christian.

Why did Jerry call Tom early in the morning?
Why did he turn to Tom in his desperate need?
Was it not because Tom had built a friendship
of love and trust?

When I heard Tom tell this experience, I
asked myself some heart-searching questions. I
wonder how many of my friends would turn to
me in their moment of desperation? Have I
built that kind of relationship with my friends
and neighbors that of all their friends, they
would call me?

I ask you, will you be the kind of true friend
that your friends will want to turn to in their
time of need?

Discussion Questions

1. In the light of Mark 1:1-12, how would
you define a true friend?

2. From this same Scripture, how would
you describe a friendship evangelist?

3. Why is it important to be sensitive to
your friends in their time of deep need?

4. What might be some practical things a
person could do to express compassion?

5. Brainstorm for a while and then list some

creative things you might do to reach your friends for Christ.

6. How much time and effort do you personally spend reaching out to your friends?

7. What spiritual gifts or natural talents do you have that you could use in friendship evangelism? How might you use them?

8. How might you and some of your fellow believers do something cooperative in friendship evangelism?

9. What do you understand it means to be "Christ-centered" in your friendship evangelism?

Chapter Two

Loving Lost People

Luke 15

As I BEGIN WRITING this chapter, Tiffany Sessions still is missing. She mysteriously disappeared from her home and has not been seen or heard from since. Millions of dollars have been spent and thousands of volunteers have given of their time in the search. Still, no Tiffany. But when Tiffany's father appeared on a segment of the "20/20" television program, Mr. Sessions continued to be very much a man obsessed with a mission: the mission of finding his daughter.

I can feel intensely Mr. Sessions's anguish and passion to find his daughter. For I myself have two daughters. And I can't help but think also of another Parent—God who suffers deep anguish over a similar but infinitely more serious loss: the eternal loss of billions of people who are dead in trespasses and sins.

Luke 15 most graphically describes God's loving concern for lost people. It reports three brief stories Jesus told about the loss of three valuable objects: a sheep, a coin and a son. The theme of Luke 15 and the thesis of this chapter is one: *God wants you to search lovingly and redemptively for lost people.*

To help you understand the full ramifications of this truth, I want to examine four threads of thought that run through Jesus' three stories: (1) lost people, (2) lethargic hearts, (3) loving search and (4) lavish celebration.

1. Lost people

Luke's introduction to the three stories puts Jesus in the center of a large crowd of people—people we might call irreligious and undesirable. (Luke identifies them as tax collectors and sinners.) They were the spiritually confused, the morally bankrupt. Conventional wisdom supposed God had no use for any of them.

Off to the side was a huddle of religious leaders. They were shaking their heads and complaining that Jesus, Who called Himself God's Son, was befriending these worthless sinners.

"This man welcomes sinners and eats with them," muttered the Pharisees and teachers of the law (Luke 15:2).

a. God, the loving Father, cares about lost people.

Jesus knew exactly what the Pharisees were thinking. He was grieved by their uncaring attitude toward lost people. He told His three graphic, unforgettable stories to portray to Pharisees, lawyers and all His audience that lost people are important and valuable to God.

It was as though Jesus was saying to those religious leaders and even to us today, "I need to clarify something for all of you. I do not want there to be any further confusion on this issue, so I'm going to tell you not once, not twice, but three times that lost people—*especially* lost people—are highly important and valuable to God!"

When it comes to evaluating their fellow beings, the non-Christian world throughout history has been little different from those caustic critics of Jesus' day. Listen to a brief sampling of what some respected writers have said regarding humankind.

- Jean Girandeaux: "Timid punctuation marks sprinkled among the incomprehensible sentences of life."
- Byron: "A degraded mass of animated dust."
- William Ralph Inge: "A poor creature halfway between an ape and a god."
- W.S. Gilbert: "Nature's sole mistake."

- Bernard of Clairvaux: "The food of worms."
- Homer: "Among all creatures that breathe on earth and crawl on it there is not anywhere a thing more dismal than man."

Atrocious descriptions of mankind, are they not? But while man may view his fellow creature with disdain and deprecation, God values man quite differently.

b. Lost people are the crowning wonder of God's creation.

People are extremely important to God! In fact, people are so valuable to Him that He Himself became one. He died for people. And He is pleased to take up residence in the hearts of redeemed people!

How much do lost people mean to you? The people who live around you, who work with you. The people whom you see where you shop, where you buy your gas, where you have your hair done. How important do you think they are to God?

c. Our love for lost people must be translated into action.

You and I can think of outstanding Christians who certainly are important to God. Billy Graham. Chuck Swindoll. Elisabeth Elliot. Your pastor. The missionaries for whom you pray.

But what about the dregs of society? The drug peddlers? The child pornographers? The greedy stockbrokers? The crooked attorneys?

Certainly Jesus' three stories about the lost sheep, the lost coin and the lost son must have caught the attention of those religious leaders as they gathered in their "holy huddle" to condemn Jesus for mixing with undesirable, sinful people. Surely they must have been touched by the love of a God Who could look beyond the sins of such people, Who said then and says today, "Although you've gone astray and become lost, I still love you. I care deeply for you. You matter very much to Me!"

You see, friendship evangelism was born in the heart of a God Who loves people. As the shepherd loved his lost sheep, as the woman loved her lost coin, as the father loved his lost son, so God more than we can measure or comprehend loves people, people who are lost, lost in trespasses and sins.

The heart of any Christian will melt with love and compassion when he or she comes to really understand that people apart from God have no hope. People without Christ the Savior are woefully, eternally lost!

Friendship evangelism will never really grip your heart until you come to understand Jesus' amazing claim, "I am the way and the truth and the life. No one comes to the Father except through me" (John 14:6).

You see, as nice as your neighbor across the

street may be, as moral as your work associates may seem, as religious as your friends and relatives may appear, if they don't know Jesus as their Savior, they are tragically and forever lost!

Peter confirmed this before the Jewish Sanhedrin. He stated categorically, "Salvation is found in no one else, for there is no other name under heaven given to men by which we must be saved" (Acts 4:12). And Paul adds to this truth when he insists, "No one can lay any foundation other than the one already laid, which is Jesus Christ" (1 Corinthians 3:11). Yes, people who are separated from God by sin and who have never trusted Him are—lost!

Pastors don't rub shoulders with non-Christians quite as often as lay people do. The lay person works side by side with unsaved people every day while the pastor necessarily spends most of his time with his flock and in his study. As a pastor, I have to work at developing non-Christian contacts and at being sensitive to non-Christians whom God brings to my office. If I am not alert, I may miss these opportunities that God brings into my life.

One morning a truck driver in his 30s came to our church office and asked to see a pastor. At that moment I was the only pastor available. When the man (we'll call him Carl) came into my office, he introduced himself and said, "I'm in a mess. I need God's help bad!"

He continued by explaining to me that he had come to church a few times with his girlfriend.

They had two children. They had been living with her parents (members of our church) for about six months. He said he was looking for a job in Omaha so he wouldn't have to be on the road so much. He had asked our elder who handles benevolences for some financial help to rent an apartment, but as yet had heard nothing about any assistance.

I called the elder and inquired about the financial request. The elder said the Benevolences Committee couldn't help because the couple wasn't married.

"Carl," I said to the trucker, "why haven't you and Karla (another fictitious name) gotten married?"

"Because Karla wants a church wedding and we can't afford it!" he explained.

"Carl, I can marry you two right here in my office if you want," I offered. He thought that would be a great idea, so I called the marriage license office and learned it would cost 10 dollars for a license and nine dollars for a blood test. He said he had that much money and would take care of the details right away.

"But before you go, let me ask you a few more questions, Carl," I said. His answers to my questions revealed clearly that he knew he was lost and without hope of eternal life. I shared with him how God loved him and had sent His Son to die for him. We prayed together, and Carl rose from his knees with a newfound joy on his face.

In the early afternoon Carl returned with Karla. My secretary, Teresa, and Debbie, another secretary at the church, witnessed the brief ceremony as I pronounced them man and wife. After it was over, I congratulated the couple.

"You can come back on Monday to get a check for your apartment," I said.

Carl said he had one more item of business. "Karla wants to get saved just like I did," he told me. I had assumed because her parents were members of our church that Karla was a believer. After I shared with her the gospel and she prayed to invite Christ into her life, I filled out a "Spiritual Birth Certificate" for her just like the one I had given to Carl.

The couple left my office full of gratitude, Carl commenting to Karla—his face aglow— "Now we can celebrate our spiritual birthday and our wedding anniversary the same day!"

Today Carl has a job driving taxis. The couple is in our church. And hopefully they will continue to grow as new babes in Christ.

That brings me to the second thread in the narrative . . .

2. Lethargic hearts

Spiritual lethargy was very evident in the watching religious leaders who muttered, "This man welcomes sinners and eats with them."

a. Religious people can be cold and calloused.

I just mentioned that as a pastor I don't have the plentiful contacts with lost people that the average layperson has. But I do travel frequently on planes and have brief opportunities to share Christ with fellow passengers.

On one such trip to Asia I had spoken to a group of missionaries in Japan and then in a seminar on evangelism for Taiwan pastors. As I boarded my flight that would take me to Tokyo, Seattle, Minneapolis and Omaha, I breathed a prayer.

"Lord," I prayed, "I've been talking a lot about personal evangelism these past few days. Would You be so kind as to let me do some of it on this flight?"

When I reached my seat, I discovered it was between two Chinese women. In good Oriental protocol, I greeted the older of the two first. She didn't respond, probably because she did not speak English. To my delight the younger woman answered in fluent English. I learned that her name was Debbie and that she was en route to Columbus, Ohio, where she was to attend Ohio State University to sharpen her English teaching skills.

After we visited awhile I learned further that she had attended a Protestant church for some time, but that finding the church "very cold and full of hypocrites," she had left, never intending to return. I assured her that not all churches were like that. I asked if I might tell her about Christ Community Church in Omaha.

She showed keen interest as I told her how Donna and I in July, 1980, had arrived in Omaha with a down payment on a house, but no furniture. The congregation, having only met me once, nevertheless joined hands and totally furnished our home for us. The love and warmth of our people touched her heart, so I went on and shared the gospel with her.

As our plane landed in Tokyo, I led Debbie in a brief prayer of commitment and gave her a spiritual birth certificate. Then, I realized that in exactly 10 days I was scheduled to be in Columbus for an Evangelism Explosion Leadership Training Clinic for pastors.

Ten days later, guess where I took my team! At the university, I had another visit with Debbie. Three of the clinicians were university staff people, and they continued to follow up Debbie, later also leading her roommate to Christ.

How sad that for some years Debbie had been turned off by cold, calloused religious people!

From Jesus' story of the lost son we also learn . . .

b. Even older brothers can be indifferent.

Jesus goes on to tell about the elder brother who was angry at the attention paid the prodigal. He complained to his father about his generosity and forgiveness.

"You never gave me even a young goat so I could celebrate with my friends. But when this son of yours who has squandered your property with prostitutes comes home, you kill the fattened calf for him!" (15:29-30). What a sad picture of lethargy toward lost humanity!

Too often the church today is so caught up with the 99 sheep that it has forgotten the 1 that is lost. The 99 are feeding sumptuously. But there is nothing for those around them who are lost.

My wife, Donna, went with Jason and Amy on a follow-up visit to a couple who had just come to Christ a week earlier. Their son was home from the University of Nebraska in Lincoln for spring break. After expressing delight in her new-found faith, the mother started to reminisce about their former church, a small mainline denominational church. Everyone in the church knew everyone else's children. They had watched them grow up. They remembered how they had participated in the church's Christmas programs.

Suddenly the son interrupted his mother. "Yeah, Mom, that was all good, but no one ever shared the gospel of Christ with us! It wasn't until some of the kids from Christ Community Church helped me a few years ago and it wasn't until these friends came to see you last week that we all found eternal life!"

How sad it is that churches, year after year, can dutifully keep the machinery running, can minister to the 99 within the fold without doing anything to reach the lost sheep or the younger brother! The point of all three stories, then, was that . . .

c. Jesus wants to make us caring people.

What is your attitude toward lost people? Are you touched by their lostness? Does your heart break for them? Do you pray for them with tears? Are you prepared to go to them with the message of hope and life? Or, like the calloused, religious leaders of Jesus' day, do you pull your righteous robes around you, ignoring Christ's mandate to seek and save the lost?

Dying people must find Christ, Who is the Life. People groping in darkness must see Him Who is the Light. Whatever the cost to us, lost people must be found!

So the real question that needs to be answered is this: What will I do to express my loving concern for the lost people close to me?

I was busy at my computer on some last minute preparations for our upcoming World Missions Festival. My secretary rang me on the intercom to ask if I could talk to a man who had come to the church office looking for a pastor to help him.

I didn't say it to Teresa, but my initial response—God forgive me—was, "Lord, don't You know I must get ready for our missions festival? Why this untimely interruption?" But I went out to meet Paul and somewhat reluctantly invited him into my office.

I learned that the man sitting across from me was a nominal Roman Catholic. His wife was a nominal Pentecostal. As a youth Paul had played baseball with a young man from our church. He had been impressed by him and by, his family's Christian testimony.

My heart almost broke as he told me how he had lost his job, how his wife had just been through eye surgery without any medical insurance because he was out of work, how their family of three had been evicted from their apartment and had been living in a motel for four days with hardly anything to eat.

I could see that Paul was not a chronic welfare case. He could have provided for his family through his part-time lawn care company, but this was early spring, and there was no grass to mow. Paul needed someone who cared. He needed someone to help. Again, I put a call through to our elder responsible for benevolences. He was away from his phone.

I suggested to Paul that while we waited for the return call, I would like to share some wonderful news with him. He listened intently as I told him that Jesus offered eternal life as a free gift.

The two of us ended up on our knees, and Paul received Christ into his life. I spent some additional time explaining from the Word of God how he could grow now in Christ. After I finished, Paul said something that amazed me: "Pastor, my uncle is a priest, but in the 20 years he has been a priest he has *never* approached me about spiritual matters. He has *never once* talked to me about eternal life!"

How many people around us are lost and without anyone to find them! How many are without anyone who cares enough to tell them about the Savior!

This brings us to the third thread running through Luke 15 . . .

3. Loving search

In each of Jesus' stories it is clearly evident that the thing or person lost was precious to the owner. The missing sheep and coin prompted an all-out search. The bereaved father spent his days watching the horizon, waiting, praying that his wayward son would return.

Jesus was really saying to the Pharisees and scribes that the irreligious crowd with whom He was associating was important to God. They were so valuable, in fact, that He—Jesus—was looking among them for lost people whom He could bring back to God. Jesus was saying that for our sakes, too. Yes, He wants everyone who calls Him Savior and Lord to join hands with Him and with each other in an all-out search for lost people in our community, at work, at our clubs and among our friends and relatives.

But a warning stands out in Christ's three stories . . .

a. It will cost you to search for lost people.

To find the lost sheep, it cost the shepherd a dangerous, painstaking trek across the mountainside. To seek and to save the lost, Jesus left His glorious, heavenly home and was born in a lowly manger. He was despised, rejected of men and died a shameful, ugly death on a Roman gibbet.

To find lost people will cost you more than you may realize. It will cost you time to build relationships, time to pray. It will cost you money to reach out to people and meet their needs. But it's worth it to see your lost friends own Jesus as Lord!

For seven years Kim prayed daily for her best friend's husband to come to Christ. She reached out to him with many loving kindnesses. Then one day, she felt the Spirit of God prompt her to take her evangelism team to visit the man. There was one problem. It was her 14-year-old trainee's turn to do the sharing. Could she take the risk and allow this young girl to present the gospel to a 29-year-old businessman for whom she had prayed so long? Then she remembered that it is the Spirit of God Who must draw a person to Christ. So she took a step of faith and turned the presentation over to the young girl. And to her amazement God did the rest! That very night her friend's husband prayed to invite Christ into his life! But it had been costly to Kim. It had cost her hours of prayer and days of reaching out to the man.

Another thing you need to remember is that . . .

b. Many lost people desperately want to be found.

Sheep are innately followers and wanderers. Although they may long for the security of the fold, they seldom, if ever, can find their way home. Hence the need for a concerned shepherd and a loving evangelist!

In Jesus' story, the lost son one day came to his senses and longed for father and home. Likewise there are scores, hundreds, thousands of lost people—many of them in your network of relationships—who deep in their hearts have "had it" with this world's pleasures. They long for something better. They're reaching—often unconsciously—after God and the satisfaction that He alone can supply. They desperately want to be found! They're waiting for someone to lovingly, redemptively reach out to them. I know, because I meet them all the time!

One morning I was checking in at the airline counter when I noticed behind me a young woman shuffling her feet and showing concern about checking in on time for her flight.

"Excuse me, ma'am," I said. "This is going to take pretty long because I'm also getting a ticket for someone else. Why don't you try the next line to speed things up?"

"Oh, it's all right," she responded cheerfully, "I'm sure we're going to the same place." When I reached my seat on the plane, sure enough, there was the woman I had talked to at the ticket counter. She was sitting by the window and I was next to the aisle.

"We meet again!" she exclaimed with a smile. "My name is Noel."

"My name is Tom," I returned. When I told her I was going to Atlanta, she said she was going on from Atlanta to Memphis. She was going to spend the weekend with her fiance who was a marine. After more time getting acquainted, I asked her if she and her husband-to-be had a good spiritual foundation for their marriage. I quoted the well-known adage that couples who *pray* together *stay* together.

My new friend showed considerable interest, so I asked her what she would say to God at heaven's gate when He asked her why He should let her in. I will never forget her fascinating response.

"Tom," she said, "there was a time when I didn't know if there *was* a God at all! So I prayed, 'God, I don't know if You really exist or not, but if You do, would You please show me unmistakably that You do!'

"That day," she continued, "I went to a department store and was standing there waiting for the elevator to come, but it was delayed for some reason. Meanwhile a man who was on a ladder painting the ceiling climbed down and came over to where I was and said, 'Young lady, I don't know who you are, but I want to tell you something. There's a God and He loves you and He has a plan for your life!'

"At that point," she said, "the elevator arrived, so I excused myself and got on. But I couldn't forget that man and what he had said. I stood there crying, because God had showed me that He really does exist!"

"Do you believe that God sent that man?" I asked her. When she told me she was absolutely convinced He did, I asked, "Do you think it's possible that God sent a second man and put him on this plane right next to you to tell you the rest of the story?"

This thought must have occurred to her, because she sat there for half an hour with her eyes as big as saucers and her mouth wide open while I shared the gospel with her. The flight attendant gave her a bag of peanuts and a Coke, but she never touched them as she listened to "the man whom God had sent."

She was a "sheep" that desperately wanted to be found. Praise God, that day on that plane God found her and ended her search for Him and for the wonderful plan He had for her life!

This thought of people desperately wanting to be found should cause each of us to learn a lesson from the shepherd of our narrative . . .

c. To search for the lost, you may have to leave the "found."

Our church hosted a seminar taught by Dann Spader entitled "How to Grow a Healthy Church." Afterward, our leaders drew up a list of our ministries and classified them under three words: win, build, equip. Our faces turned bright red when we discovered how few of our ministries intentionally sought to win people to Christ. And that for a church that prided itself in being a "Great Commission church"! The allocation of our funds and personnel revealed the same imbalance.

So we are presently trying to motivate and equip more of our people to become involved in reaching out to their friends, relatives, associates and neighbors. As a pastor, I am seeking to model what I teach, by getting more involved with non-Christians. I joined a tennis club and began praying systematically for my tennis buddies.

One day one of them, Gordon, visited our church, but I didn't recognize him. And believe it or not, he didn't recognize me! We were so used to seeing one another in our sweaty tennis outfits that we were caught off guard by business suits and ties. Knowing the man was a visitor, I called on him the next day at his home. I asked how he kept so fit, and he told me he played tennis. When I inquired where, it turned out to be the same

club where I played. Suddenly to the embarrassment of us both we recognized each
other!

That evening something eternal happened in
his life. And a few weeks later I had the joy of
baptizing Gordon!

To find lost sheep we have to leave the safety
of the sheepfold. We have to leave the 99 and
go on a loving search. Why don't you do a little
personal inventory right now and ask yourself,
"What does it cost me to win my lost friends to
Christ? What new sacrifices am I willing to
make to reach out to them with the love of
Christ?"

Searching for lost people in primitive lands
can be quite costly. Ask the missionaries who
are doing it. But in our own country and culture it also can be costly. Yet seeing our lost
friends come to know Christ is truly worth all
the inconvenience, pain and sacrifice. In fact, it
is something to really rejoice about! That leads
us to the fourth thread running through the
Luke 15 narrative . . .

4. Lavish celebration

When something of great value is lost, be it a
sheep, a coin or a son, there is great sorrow.
But when, at last, the lost is found, there is
great rejoicing! The greater the value of the ob-
ject, the more lavish the celebration! Notice in
Jesus' three stories that . . .

a. When lost people are found, they celebrate!

Certainly the lost son rejoiced when he found himself home safe and sound, comfortable and cared for with father and family! Can you imagine how his heart leaped with joy and gladness? I doubt that he ever stopped smiling until, late that first night, he fell asleep warm and contented in his very own bed!

And when he awakened the next morning and sat across from his dad at breakfast eating his favorite cereal, he may have had to blink and pinch himself to see if he wasn't still dreaming. It was too good to be true!

A few weeks ago in Sunday morning worship at our church we celebrated the baptism of several new believers. As is our practice, we gave each person an opportunity to share a brief testimony. It was the high point of our service. One person after another, face aglow, gave praise to God for the way Christ had saved him or her. No two testimonies were alike. One young man said that his baptism was on the occasion of his first spiritual birthday: one year earlier to the day, he had trusted Christ as his Savior! The congregation broke into loud applause as together in great rejoicing we entered into his joy.

Rising from the waters of baptism, another person shouted spontaneously, "Praise be to God!" A third told how at last year's Easter musical she had trusted Christ for eternal life. Again, the congregation broke into loud applause and praise to God!

Is there any joy like the joy of a sinner totally forgiven, completely cleansed after a lifetime away from God? Is there any happiness like that of a person, lost in darkness and despair, now exposed to the radiance of God's glory and grace in the Person of Jesus Christ? The lost has been *found*!

b. When lost people are found, the church also celebrates!

The shepherd finds his wandering sheep, returns to the fold and with great joy "throws a party." The woman finds her lost coin and gathers her friends and neighbors for a time of celebration. The father welcomes home his wayward son and calls for a robe, a ring, sandals, the fattened calf and unprecedented rejoicing. In the same way God's people celebrate over the salvation of each valuable person.

Since seventh grade, teenager Geoff had prayed for his classmate Cassy. Finally, after four years of praying and an EE course in sharing the gospel effectively, Geoff took three other young friends—Cheryl, Sheena and Dana—to visit Cassy in her home. For the first time since Geoff had known Cassy she listened carefully and responsively. When they returned to the church that night, the four young evangelists were overjoyed to report that Cassy had at last transferred her trust from religion to Jesus Christ. There was applause and boisterous cheering from the rest of the youth and adults in the classroom in the wonderful news that Cassy, like a lost sheep, had been brought into the fold.

c. When lost people are found, heaven celebrates!

Twice in Luke 15 Jesus says that there is heavenly rejoicing "over one sinner who repents" (15:7, 10).

Did you know that when you trusted Christ as Savior, whether at age 7, 17 or 70, all heaven erupted in glorious praise? Are you aware that when your name was announced to the angels from one end of heaven to the other, singing and shouting such as earth has never heard broke forth? God was praised. Jesus was glorified and all heaven celebrated when you, like the lost son, returned to Father and home.

A few years ago I found it necessary to go to a weight-control center and sign up for a weight reduction program. Every day on the way home from the office, I dropped by the center to weigh in and report my reduction progress. And each day I built a friendly relationship with Betty, my diet counselor.

Several years earlier I had written up my personal testimony in tract format telling of my helicopter escape April 30, 1975, from the roof of the U.S. embassy in Saigon, Vietnam. I used the story of my escape to illustrate God's question: "How shall we escape if we ignore such a great salvation?" (Hebrews 2:3)—the salvation being that which comes through Jesus Christ.

One day as I weighed in at the center I felt led to give a copy of my testimony to Betty. The next day she asked for another copy to give to her fiancé. She said they both were very interested in what I had to say.

The following day she asked for the address of my church. She promised the two of them would visit us on Sunday.

On Monday when I stopped at the center, Betty wasn't there. She had gone home early, but the other diet counselor had a little red book, *Partners in Growing,* that Betty had left with her. "Betty is asking if you would sign the certificate in the front," the diet counselor said.

In the front of the booklet is a spiritual birth certificate which new believers sign when they place their trust in Christ. Evidently Betty had trusted Christ as her Savior following our Sunday morning service, had received the booklet, but hadn't had any witness available to sign the certificate.

How I rejoiced that day to learn of Betty's newly found faith in Christ! But how much more celebration took place in celestial realms as Betty's name was announced from one end of heaven to the other!

Betty married her fiance and settled down in

a little town in western Nebraska. I often wondered what happened to her. Then not long ago she called me to say she had moved back to Omaha and would be coming to Christ Community Church again. My heart rejoiced. I had lost track of Betty, but God had not, and she was continuing her relationship with Him!

That's the heart of an evangelist rejoicing over a lost person who has been found. That is the thrill of the shepherd who knows his lost sheep has been returned safely to the fold. And that is a little glimpse of the excitement that must be felt in the courts of heaven every time another person comes to Christ!

Let me ask again: What is your attitude toward lost people? I hope you are not cold and calloused like the religious leaders of Christ's day—indifferent to lost people around you. I hope you are not passively avoiding Christ's eternally significant mandate to seek and save the lost.

Do you really understand that people without Christ are lost? Does your heart break over their lostness? Do you pray for them with tears? Are you prepared to go to them with the message of hope and life?

Let me lovingly and urgently remind you that dying people must find Christ the Life! People groping in darkness must see Him who alone is the Light! Lost people, whatever the cost, must be found!

So the real question that you need to answer

is this: What will I do to express my loving concern for the lost people close about me?

Let me suggest four steps which you can take immediately. I'll call them Action Steps:

1. Develop a list of lost people in your network of relationships and start praying for them daily.

2. Begin building bridges to them by regularly expressing love and concern for them in tangible, helpful, practical ways.

3. Look for opportunities to invite them to the next visitor-friendly event at your church.

4. As the Lord presents the opportunity, share with them your testimony and the good news of Jesus Christ.

Remember, people—lost people—matter to God! And He wants you to do everything possible to search for them, to find them and to bring them into His saving grace!

Discussion Questions

1. What are three Bible verses that set forth Christ as the only way to God and eternal life?

2. If eternal life is found in Christ alone, what does that say about people who don't know Him or are not trusting Him as their Savior?

3. According to the Scriptures, what does it really mean to be "lost"?

4. How do you think knowing that your friends, relatives and neighbors are lost might motivate you?

5. Why do you think the Pharisees were unconcerned about tax collectors and sinners?

6. What impact do you think Jesus intended His three stories recorded in Luke 15 to have on the religious leaders of His day? What impact on believers today?

Chapter Three

Expanding Your Vision

Acts 18:1-11

PEOPLE GENERALLY GO where they *look.* They are influenced to action by what they *view* with intensity.

New York Yankee baseball star Mickey Mantle visited Omaha on a promotional trip to advertise a well-known product. While at one of Omaha's large shopping malls, he was autographing baseballs for his fans and admirers. As Mickey signed young Tommy's ball, the little lad asked, "Mister Mantle, can you tell me how you can hit so many baseballs for home runs? How do you get the ball to go over the fence so many times?"

"Well, young man," Mickey replied, "first you have to see it happen in your mind. You have to visualize it going over the fence. Then, when you get up to bat, you just keep thinking and seeing it going over the fence. And sure enough, when you hit the ball squarely it goes flying over the wall!"

It has been said that our eyes are the windows to our souls. Our eyes influence our lives profoundly. What people look at with intensity greatly affects their actions.

It has been observed that at night drivers who focus on the headlights of vehicles coming toward them will be drawn like a magnet in the direction of the oncoming traffic. This sometimes results in head-on collisions.

Advertisers know that if they can visualize their product on television often enough and attractively enough, a number of viewers are going to pull out their checkbooks or reach for their wallets to buy!

In Acts 18:9-10, we see that Christ knows better than anyone the power of visualization. He visualizes our cities not as brick and mortar, but as *people*:

> One night the Lord spoke to Paul in a vision: "Do not be afraid; keep on speaking, do not be silent. For I am with you, and no one is going to attack and harm you, because I have many people in this city."

Christ said that He had many people in Corinth. They were people whom, according in

Ephesians 1:4-7, God the Father chose before the foundation of the world—people whom Christ the Son had purchased with His own blood.

But as amazing as Christ's selection process was and as powerful as His saving grace is, if those people were going to be impacted for eternity, He still needed Paul and others to share the wonderful news of the gospel with them. Note again Jesus' command to Paul: "Do not be afraid; keep on speaking, do not be silent."

It's the same today. Christ looks over your city or town and sees people whom God the Father has selected, people whom He the Son died to save. And He wants to give you a *vision* of your city or town—not as streets and shops, houses and land, but as *people* who need to hear of His saving grace.

If you lack vision, people all around you will perish eternally.

But you ask, "What's the vision like that Christ wants me to catch?" I see in Paul's vision a five-part vision for you: tentmaking, teamwork, testimony, target and teaching. Let's take a closer look at this five-point vision.

1. Tentmaking

Notice that tentmaking provided Paul with both an occupation and an opportunity. It was both a chance to work and a chance to witness.

a. Occupation

Each of us needs to have a means to support ourselves, but it shouldn't be our chief focus. For Paul, support meant making tents:

> After this, Paul left Athens and went to Corinth. There he met a Jew named Aquila, a native of Pontus, who had recently come from Italy with his wife Priscilla, because Claudius had ordered all the Jews to leave Rome. Paul went to see them, and because he was a tentmaker as they were, he stayed and worked with them. (Acts 18:1-3)

Paul, like most of us today, had to work hard to keep food on the table, clothes on his back and a roof over his head. It is great to be visionary, but we still need to provide for the necessities of life. In one of his letters to the Corinthians Paul writes, "We work hard with our own hands" (1 Corinthians 4:12). Later in the same letter Paul asks, "Is it only I and Barnabas who must work for a living?" (9:6).

Things have not greatly changed in more than 19 centuries. Much of what we do in any given day is aimed at sustaining physical life. While such occupation is necessary, we must be careful that it doesn't consume all of our time, energy and interest. Some Christians pour all their life into their jobs, as if that were all there is. Others pour all of their income from their jobs into temporal things, as if temporal things were going to last forever.

Paul reminded the Corinthians that on the day of judgment their work would be tested by fire (1 Corinthians 3:12-16). The "wood, hay or straw" would go up in smoke; the "gold, silver, costly stones" would survive. Paul saw people and his ministry to them as his most important occupation. He writes to the Corinthians, "Are you not the result of my work in the Lord? . . . You are the seal of my apostleship" (9:1-2). Eternal work is people, because only people are eternal. Therefore, Paul and the Corinthians were to focus their real efforts upon winning and discipling people.

Jack is a very committed lay leader in our church who has been well equipped in evangelism and has trained many other lay people. But more importantly, evangelism and winning people to Christ have become a way of life for Jack.

Recently in his office Jack met with another businessman to close the purchase of additional office space in a building adjacent to his facility. Upon completing the sale, Jack turned to his friend and asked him some questions regarding his spiritual orientation. Jack found that the man was searching for answers and really wanted to prepare for eternity.

Jack patiently and with great sensitivity led his friend through the gospel and a commitment to Jesus Christ as Savior and Lord. He encouraged him to become involved in a strong Bible-teaching church and he gave him some initial counsel on how to grow in his new-found faith.

It is exciting to see that Jack's business is both a means for supporting his family and an arena where he can witness for Christ. One day after he led his first person to Christ he said to me, "Tom, this is far more exciting than the biggest computer sale my business equipment company has ever made!"

I like the way a Christian baker put it when he was asked what his work was: "My work is people, but I bake bread to pay expenses." Paul's work was people, but he made tents to pay expenses. Let me ask you: Is your work all "tentmaking," or are there some people whom you are impacting for God and eternity?

b. Opportunity

Your place of employment may prove to be your greatest arena for witness. We are not informed for sure, but it is certainly possible that Aquila and Priscilla were not Christian believers when Paul first entered into his partnership with them. While they worked together making tents, Paul may have introduced Aquila and Priscilla to Christ Jesus.

Of one thing I am sure: Paul used those hours of work to disciple these two choice people and prepare them for a wider Christian ministry. When Paul finally left Corinth, we are informed that he was "accompanied by Priscilla and Aquila" (Acts 18:18), whom he left at Ephesus (18:19) while he continued on to Caesarea and Antioch (18:21-22). In Ephesus, Aquila and Priscilla not only prepared the ground for Paul's later ministry there but had the important privilege of instructing the zealous but inadequately informed Apollos.

Wherever Paul was he saw opportunity to witness. And whether under Caesar's praetorian guard (Philippians 1:13) or in the home of Aquila and Priscilla, he was actively introducing people to Jesus.

Wayne is another member of our church who views his place of employment as a venue for both work and witness. Wayne is very careful not to allow his witness to interfere with his work, lest his employer be offended. So he looks for opportunities at coffee or lunch breaks to share his faith. A good number of his fellow welders have come to Christ.

One day over lunch he was talking with an associate about the things of Christ. Another worker sitting close by complained.

"All you guys ever talk about is heaven and God and the Bible. Why don't you quit talking about all that nonsense?"

Wayne replied in a very unorthodox way but specially phrased to shock the man into his senses: "You think our talk is nonsense because you're going to hell. We're going to heaven and so we like to talk about it! If you don't like our talk, you can go eat your lunch somewhere else!" Strangely enough, the man didn't move, but continued to eat there, listening quietly.

Several days later he asked Wayne if they could talk after work. As they sat together in Wayne's car, the man said to Wayne, "I've been thinking about what you said. I don't want to go to hell. Can you tell me what I have to do?"

Wayne's approach was not one I would recommend, but in that instance God used it to awaken the welder to his need of a Savior. And Wayne praised God again for the opportunity his place of employment gave him to witness.

Has your place of employment become both a temporal and an eternal workshop? Are you using your place of business as a bridge to reach people for Christ? One day when your "tents" all go up in smoke, will there be any people that you personally impacted for God?

2. Teamwork

Like Jesus, Paul had a vision of teamwork. He endeavored to build an effective team that could work and witness with him wherever he went. On his teams he had room for both new and veteran workers.

a. New believers

Even if Aquila and Priscilla were believers before Paul met them at Corinth (Acts 18:2), they likely were young in the faith. Yet Paul

confidently allowed them to accompany him to
Ephesus and, with like confidence, left them in
Ephesus (18:18-19) for such ministry as they
might have until he could return there. As I
noted above, Aquila and Priscilla had at least
one very significant contact in the person of
Apollos, inviting this zealous, effective disciple
into their home, where they "explained to him
the way of God more adequately" (18:26).

New Christians can help you reach their lost
friends. From the above verses it is clear that
Paul invited some new believers to join him in
evangelism. Someone has said, "Lead me to a
new believer and I'll show you a whole nest of
responsive sinners."

A young man named Scott led Sharon to
Christ. Seven days later he went back to visit
Sharon and met Don and Jean. When Scott
shared the gospel with them, they too came to
Christ. Seven days later Scott returned again to
find Karen and Kirby visiting Sharon. They too
listened to the gospel and trusted Christ for
eternal life.

The author of Acts tells us that "many of the
Corinthians who heard [Paul] believed and
were baptized." (18:8). I can't help but believe
that some of them were friends, neighbors or
relatives of Paul's team members, Priscilla and
Aquila.

We need to be careful to help people we lead
to Christ to develop a witness to their families,
friends and neighbors. Sometimes we will train

them to share their faith. Other times we may simply go with them to share with their non-christian friends and relatives.

b. Veteran workers

The Scriptures inform us that "when Silas and Timothy came from Macedonia, Paul devoted himself exclusively to preaching, testifying to the Jews that Jesus was the Christ" (18:5).

There should be no "loners" in the work of Christ. We simply can't do it alone. Christ didn't! Paul didn't!

We need to determine how other fellow believers with their differing gifts can complement our witness. Some have gifts of hospitality, helps, teaching, mercy, wisdom, knowledge. Paul says he planted the seed, Apollos watered it and God brought about a harvest (1 Corinthians 3:6). Even so we will find that through cooperative efforts, we'll be a lot more fruitful in our witness.

Some people in the church look to the pastor as the "big gun"—the experienced evangelist to whom they can refer all their unsaved relatives and friends. They believe he is best equipped to witness and to win. But it is very encouraging to a pastor to have other trained, effective evangelists in the church who can be tapped when needed.

One day I received a phone call from a stranger. Jack was not a member of our church, but he had heard that God was using our church to win people to Christ.

"Pastor," he said, "my wife is in the hospital at death's door and doesn't know Christ. I've tried unsuccessfully for many years to win her to Christ. Would you be able to come and talk to her?"

I could see that it was urgent, so I jumped in my car and rushed to the hospital. By the time I arrived, Jack's wife was in a coma. I left my card with a note explaining to Jack that I had been too late.

Jack called me back and said the doctors assured him they could bring his wife out of the coma one more time before she expired. When could I come?

I called Annie, a woman in our church who is well trained and has a compassion for people who are hurting. She promised me that she would stay near her phone every day until Jack called her.

When the doctors revived Jack's wife, he called Annie and in a few moments she was by the bedside of the dying woman. Annie reached out to her with love and tender care. When the right moment presented itself she shared the gospel and led the dying woman to Christ.

But Jack's wife didn't die as soon as the doctors expected. For two or three days she remained conscious, reading the Scriptures, singing hymns with her family and rejoicing that God had now prepared her for her heavenly home!

How wonderful that God had gifted Annie for witnessing and given her an available heart! How pleased I am to have someone like her whom I can call on to help me with the evangelistic opportunities that arise from time to time!

3. Testimony

The vision to win the "many people in this city" (Acts 18:10) must be communicated. In Corinth the gospel was communicated both by reasoning and by testifying. While each of these methods has its place, sometimes one is more effective than the other.

a. Reasoning

"Every Sabbath [Paul] reasoned in the synagogue, trying to persuade Jews and Greeks" (18:4).

The gospel, of course, is very reasonable. We should always be prepared to answer everyone who asks us to give the reason for the hope that we have (1 Peter 3:15). But reasoning doesn't always persuade people to trust Christ. It seems evident that few, if any, of those attending the synagogue came to Christ.

b. Testifying

"When Silas and Timothy came from Macedonia, Paul devoted himself exclusively to preaching, testifying to the Jews that Jesus was the Christ" (18:5).

Testimony to our firsthand experience of Christ's grace ofttimes is more powerful than logic. Reasoning seems to focus more on objective truth or doctrine, while testimony relates to personal, subjective experience.

Testimony is a very prominent ingredient in advertising. How often we see some well-known sports figure promoting tennis shoes, deodorant, beverages or breakfast cereal. God likewise uses the power of personal testimony for His purposes. Many times I have seen a prospect's whole attitude change when confronted by a sincere testimony of God's saving grace.

For two evenings Judy and her two friends, without success, had shared the gospel with Edmund. Finally, Judy asked if Edmund would be willing to go with her to the pastor. The pastor, sensing Edmund had heard a lot of doctrine, suggested that the team join him in sharing their personal testimonies. Suddenly Edmund rose to his feet.

"I'm convinced!" Edmund exclaimed. "This is what I want. Pray for me at once!" Testimony accomplished what extensive reasoning could not do.

4. Target

According to Acts 18:10, Paul's objective was people. But where would he find them? And in the interest of effectiveness, on which people should he focus his time and energy? Paul seemed to aim at two targets: people at worship and people at home.

There are situations where the church sanctuary is a very appropriate place to witness. Some churches hold evangelistic meetings aimed expressly at non-Christians. At Christ Community Church weddings, funerals, special Christmas and Easter events are appropriate occasions for sharing the gospel.

One funeral stands out in my mind as a classic opportunity for evangelism. Jim had been one of our best personal evangelists. When he died his wife, Margaret, asked the coroner to place his EE two-question-mark pin on the lapel of his suit. As friends and family walked past the casket many of them paid special attention to the two question marks, wondering what they represented.

In his funeral sermon our senior pastor, Robert Thune, made reference to the two questions and, in fact, asked those present to answer the questions silently. Then he presented the gospel as Jim would have wanted him to share it. He invited any who desired to trust Christ to pray silently in their hearts after him. Finally, while their heads were still bowed, he asked for a show of hands of those who had so trusted Christ. Ten persons raised their hands!

You may ask what such a funeral service has to do with friendship evangelism. Jim had

befriended or cultivated relationships with almost everyone present that day. He had lived
Christ before them. He had shared the gospel
with many of them. He planted many seed
thoughts in their hearts. Pastor Bob was used
of God to gather in some of the harvest.

a. Church

> Every Sabbath [Paul] reasoned in
> the synagogue, trying to persuade
> Jews and Greeks.
> When Silas and Timothy came from
> Macedonia, Paul devoted himself ex-
> clusively to preaching, testifying to
> the Jews that Jesus was the Christ. But
> when the Jews opposed Paul and be-
> came abusive, he shook out his clothes
> in protest and said to them, "Your
> blood be on your own heads! I am
> clear of my responsibility. From now
> on I will go to the Gentiles" (18:4-6).

The place of worship is not necessarily the
best place for witness. It seems Paul ran into a
bees' nest of abuse and resistance at the
synagogue. The worshipers would not hear the
Truth he was presenting. So Paul left the
synagogue and went to . . .

b. Homes

> Then Paul left the synagogue and

went next door to the house of Titus
Justus, a worshiper of God. Crispus,
the synagogue ruler, and his entire
household believed in the Lord; and
many of the Corinthians who heard him
believed and were baptized (18:7-8).

As I have said, there are times when church is
a very good place for witnessing. But Christians need to get out of the fishbowl and into
the sea, out of the saltshaker and into the world
of people.

For three years British preacher Richard Baxter delivered from his pulpit polished sermons
that were marked by zeal and authority. Yet he
saw little result.

"Oh, God," Baxter prayed, "You must do
something with these people or I shall die!"

In response, God seemed to say to him, "Baxter, you have put forth your best efforts in the
wrong place. You have expected revival to
come through the church. Now try the home!"

Baxter began systematically calling in the
homes of his parish and spending entire evenings with families. Before long, revival fires
burned brightly, spreading through the
church, and from the church to the community
around.

If you want to impact your community for
Christ, you too must break out of the four walls
of your sanctuary. You must creatively and
lovingly take the good news of Jesus Christ to

the spiritually hungry families in your neighborhoods.

Notice the two words *house* (18:7) and
household (18:8). They are translations of two
Greek words, *oikia* and *oikos*, both referring in
usage not only to a dwelling but to the extended family, including domestics and even
friends, who frequented it.

It is significant that Crispus *and his entire
household* believed in the Lord. In evangelism
we sometimes use the term FRAN—*f*riends,
*r*elatives, *a*ssociates and *n*eighbors—to include
the entire group. Today, as in New Testament
times, the home is the most responsive and
fruitful target for evangelism.

The American Church Growth Institute did a
survey of 15,000 Christians to ask who was the
principal witness influencing their decision for
Christ. Seventy-five to 90 percent of those sur-
veyed, depending on where the survey was
done, pointed to a relative or friend.

The results of this research mirror the New
Testament pattern. The majority of the first
century Christians seem to have been most impacted by those in their networks of trust
relationships.

Why is a non-Christian more likely to be won
to Jesus by a friend or relative than by a
stranger? Among other reasons, five principal
ones stand out:

1. The gospel is presented by someone the

person already trusts.

2. The sharing can be unhurried and natural.

3. The witness' life-style, known to the non-Christian, adds credibility to what he or she says.

4. As a friend or relative, the witness can naturally nurture the new believer.

5. The witness' church can provide effective assistance in follow-up and assimilation.

5. Teaching

Paul gave a year and a half of his life to teach and build up the new believers at Corinth. He didn't move on to another field of service until he felt certain the Corinthian Christians could stand on their own feet and get on without him.

a. Perseverance

"So Paul stayed for a year and a half" (18:11).

As with Paul, so your follow-up of new believers will take much time. In the physical realm the same parent who gives birth normally is responsible for the nurture of that new life. Just as it takes much time to raise children, so it takes many hours, weeks and even years to bring a new babe in Christ to maturity.

When a child falls down, breaks something

or misbehaves, we don't abandon him or her. Likewise, you need to persevere in your spiritual "child care." Do not become discouraged and quit just because the spiritual babe doesn't progress at the pace you feel appropriate.

Bob had a vital part in Doug and Lori's coming to Christ. As their spiritual "parent," he sensed a responsibility for their nurture in Christ. Thus he didn't *send* them to the New Beginnings class. Rather he *accompanied* them to the class! In fact, he sat with and helped them through all seven lessons. He also sat with them in the morning worship service. He assisted them as they searched for Scripture portions and hymns. He explained to them the free-will offerings. He generally made them comfortable in what was to them the rather foreign environment of a Protestant worship service.

Bob persevered with Doug and Lori.

b. God's Word

"... Teaching them the Word of God" (18:11).

New believers need plenty of the "milk" and "meat" of God's Word. Notice that Paul taught them the Word of God. There is nothing that will cause new Christians to grow like a steady diet of God's Word. At first, they should be encouraged to read and study the simpler books of the Bible like the Gospels, Acts, First John and James.

A plumber, Jack, and his wife with their family visited our church and were led to Christ by one of our visitation evangelism teams. The whole family enrolled in our seven-week New Beginnings class. Although their children were comfortable joining our youth group, Jack and his wife didn't feel ready to get into an adult Sunday school Bible study. The weekly expositions from various parts of the Bible were a little advanced for them. So we organized a special "Grow" class for them, taking them through some of the Bible studies published by the Navigators.

Then they enrolled in our evangelism training and began sharing with their friends. Today Jack has become an elder in charge of buildings and grounds and is himself a teacher in our New Beginnings class.

Gradually as Jack and his wife mature, we will encourage them to read and study some of the more meaty Bible passages—the Letters, for example—and also the Old Testament books. We may also want to suggest that they get into a good solid weeknight Bible study.

It's a great thrill to lead friends, relatives, associates and neighbors to Christ; it is even more exciting to see them mature in their faith and walk with Christ.

Let me ask in conclusion: What kind of a vision do you have for *your* city? Is it a five-dimensional vision that includes your workplace, your extended "household"? Does it involve other Christians? Is your testimony up-to-date and convincing? Are you prepared for the necessary follow-up?

Just as God used Paul, the tentmaking witness, may God use you as you witness to friends, relatives, associates, neighbors.

Discussion Questions

1. What is your understanding of the term "the power of visualization"? In what way does what you *see* impact on what you *do*?

2. Describe what you understand "vision" to mean both in biblical terms and in our day.

3. Is it reasonable to expect the average believer in the pew to experience vision?

4. What do you understand the 20th century equivalent of a *tentmaker* to be? How might this concept be applied to your life and work?

5. Why do you think it's important to see friendship evangelism as teamwork? How might you team up with other Christians in friendship evangelism?

6. Why do you think the use of testimony is an important ingredient in friendship evangelism? What aspect of God's saving grace in your life might He use to impact the lives of your non-Christian friends?

7. What was Paul's strategy for targeting the city of Corinth? How might that strategy apply to reaching your city for Christ?

8. From Paul's strategy for nurturing new believers, what two biblical principles relate to follow-up? How might you apply those principles to your friendship evangelism?

Chapter Four

Discovering the Right Approach

Mark 5:1-20; 7:31-8:10

IN 1975, JOHN F. SOPER OF Fulton, New York, began his first pastoral ministry. His assignment: to plant a Christian and Missionary Alliance church in Bridgeton, New Jersey.

Having had no training in starting a new church, John approached the task with trepidation. After two and a half years, however, he had a congregation of 65—a creditable piece of work. But one thing greatly bothered John. All his congregation were "transfer" Christians; not one of them had come to Christ under his ministry. He had preached faithfully, he had knocked on many doors, he had done everything possible to win people to Christ. But nothing had happened!

To make matters worse, John was asked to start a church in another New Jersey community, Pomona. Reluctantly he accepted the appointment. "I'll go," he said to God, "but You will have to show me how people come to Christ."

John Soper found his answer as he meditated on Mark 5:1-20 and Mark 7:31-8:10—the Scriptures I am using as a base for this chapter. His finding: *The gospel spreads most effectively across an existing network of trust relationships.*

In the fifth chapter of Mark, the formerly demented man seemed to live his life in superlatives. A legion of demons produced great antisocial behavior. Jesus' great deliverance resulted in a great change for the better. The man's request to join Jesus' retinue issued in a great personal commission that would have great results.

Jesus' admonition to the formerly deranged, demon-possessed man is central to this chapter's theme. The wonderfully healed man wanted to be a part of Jesus' entourage. Jesus vetoed the idea. He said to the man, "Go home to your family and tell them how much the Lord has done for you, and how he has had mercy on you" (Mark 5:19).

I want to try to sort out the applicable lessons for us as we look at five "greats" that catch our attention in these Scriptures.

1. A great need

> [Jesus and His disciples] went across the lake to the region of the Gerasenes. When Jesus got out of the boat, a man with an evil spirit came from the tombs to meet him. This man lived in the tombs, and no one could bind him any more, not even with a chain. For he had often been chained hand and foot, but he tore the chains apart and broke the irons on his feet. No one was strong enough to subdue him. Night and day among the tombs and in the hills he would cry out and cut himself with stones.
>
> When he saw Jesus from a distance, he ran and fell on his knees in front of him. (Mark 5:1-6)

Jesus and His disciples had gone by boat southeast across the Sea of Galilee to an area called the Decapolis or 10 Cities. The 10 cities were essentially Greek but subject to Roman taxation and military service, and one of them, located near the steep slopes of a mountain leading down to the sea, was named Gadara. When Jesus and His disciples got out of the boat, they were immediately accosted by a man from Gadara who had a great need.

a. The Gadarene was enslaved by Satan.

The man from Gadara was not simply deranged mentally; he was mastered by Satan and possessed by demons. He lived among the tombs. Many of the tombs of that day were hewn like caves out of the side of the limestone hills. They could be lived in. But this man *had* to live in them. Being so violent, he was an outcast from his family and city.

While serving as a missionary in Vietnam in the early 1970s, I was invited to preach the gospel at the Truong Minh Gian Evangelical Church. When I arrived to preach and walked into the chapel, I felt an unusual oppression from Satan. I am not one who sees demons behind every tree or in every adverse situation. But that night I sensed that Satan was definitely seeking to hinder the preaching of the gospel.

So I prayed. "Lord God," I said, "I claim the covering of Your Son's blood." Then turning to the darkness, I addressed my foe: "Satan," I commanded, "in the strong and powerful name of Jesus Christ, I order you to depart from this place!"

Immediately I felt deep peace. I went ahead with my message. At the end I gave an invitation. One sincere seeker came forward and gave his heart to Jesus Christ. It was a glorious victory and God was praised.

b. He was like walking death.

Satan and his emissaries have one major objective for mankind: destruction. They must have been particularly satisfied with the job they were doing on the Gadarene. Not only was he "dead in . . . transgressions and sins" (Ephesians 2:1), as is every unregenerated person, but he was compulsively injuring himself physically. Likely he had injured others as well.

c. He was crying out for help.

Unclothed and uncared for, the Gadarene had fallen into the condition of a savage. He may have had a home, but to all intents and purposes he was homeless, leading a vagrant life. Victimized by Satan, he was unable to help himself.

Bob, one of my missionary colleagues in Vietnam, described an encounter he had with the power of evil spirits while he was a student at Crown College in Minnesota. Bob and a group of students regularly visited a Native American village to witness. But none of the villagers responded to the gospel.

Instead, Bob and the students felt an uncanny opposition from Satan and his demons. One day the battle came to a head when one of the women gave signs of being demon possessed. While the students didn't have a lot of experience with evil spirits, they did know that in the name of Jesus Christ they could overcome the devil.

So in the name of Christ they commanded the evil spirits, one after another, to leave the woman. The last demon to be exorcised called itself "the demon that is opposing the gospel in—" and it named the village where the students were trying to witness. The woman was clearly delivered and the students continued to return to evangelize the village. Suddenly they had a good response to their witness. A large number of the villagers gave their hearts to Christ. Those students had encountered the same demonic forces Jesus met in the first century.

d. He brought his need to Jesus.

No one has the ability to save himself or herself. He or she is powerless to break the bonds of slavery and Satan. God alone has that authority. He broke the bonds of sin and Satan in the first Christian century. He can break the bonds of sin in our day as well.

Some of earth's neediest people are those who are bound by substance abuse. Jeff was a prime example.

Through the witness of one of our EE teams, Jeff was gloriously saved. God delivered him from drugs, including alcohol, that had bound him for many years.

After completing our New Beginnings class, Jeff enrolled in EE so he could equip himself to reach his old friends and his family members for Christ.

Before long he had built up enough confidence to start sharing the gospel with them. One day he asked if his team members could call on the wife of one of his former gang members. The woman was in the hospital and close to death. As the team entered the hospital room they encountered the woman's husband—a convicted criminal who was about to be readmitted to prison. This husband asked everyone to leave the room so Jeff and his friends could talk to his wife. And that very evening the woman gave her heart to Christ!

Jesus met Jeff's need. Jesus met the need of the wife of one of Jeff's former gang members. And in the weeks that followed, Jesus met the needs of many others from Jeff's background.

Every person who has not yet met Jesus is in need of . . .

2. A great miracle

Certainly the Gadarene among the tombs was a candidate for a miracle. And the Scriptures testify that Jesus did not disappoint him.

> When he saw Jesus from a distance, he ran and fell on his knees in front of him. He shouted at the top of his voice, "What do you want with me, Jesus, Son of the Most High God? Swear to God that you won't torture me!" For Jesus had said to him, "Come out of this man, you evil spirit!"

Then Jesus asked him, "What is your name?"

"My name is Legion," he replied, "for we are many." And he begged Jesus again and again not to send them out of the area.

A large herd of pigs was feeding on the nearby hillside. The demons begged Jesus, "Send us among the pigs; allow us to go into them." He gave them permission, and the evil spirits came out and went into the pigs. The herd, about two thousand in number, rushed down the steep bank into the lake and were drowned.

Those tending the pigs ran off and reported this in the town and countryside, and the people went out to see what had happened. When they came to Jesus, they saw the man who had been possessed by the legion of demons, sitting there, dressed and in his right mind; and they were afraid. Those who had seen it told the people what had happened to the demon-possessed man—and told about the pigs as well. Then the people began to plead with Jesus to leave their region. (Mark 5:6-17)

It is interesting to note that when the demons encountered Jesus Christ they recognized that . . .

a. Jesus is God.

The Scriptures inform us that the demons believe in God and tremble (James 1:19). Here we see that they acknowledged the deity of Jesus Christ. They knew when they met Jesus that He was no mere teacher or prophet. He was—and is—God! And as God . . .

b. He is more powerful than Satan.

By His power Jesus commanded the demons to come out of the enslaved man. Greater is He Who is in us than he who is in the world! Christ is Victor over all principalities and powers. Satan is a defeated foe. Jesus exhibited His mighty power that glorious day, exorcising the demons from the wretched man and permitting them to enter the nearby herd of some 2,000 pigs. The demons promptly destroyed the pigs by driving them into the sea.

It is not difficult to imagine the consternation of those herding the pigs. Quite apart from the phenomenon of seeing 2,000 squealing, demented pigs rush down the slope and drown in the sea, the herders had their own necks to worry about. They were not only suddenly jobless, but the owners of the herd could have held them responsible for what had happened. They wasted no time getting to town to notify the owners.

c. People were curious and furious.

Such an event in Gadara was front page news! The citizenry, filled with curiosity, hurried to the scene. The owners of the pigs were more than just curious; they were furious!

The human result of Christ's miracle-working power was seated next to Jesus, "dressed and in his right mind." But when it is a contest between a person's financial interests and spiritual healing, guess which side usually wins.

d. They rejected the Savior.

The material loss of the pigs was far more significant to the people of Gadara than the spiritual triumph and glorious healing of their troubled fellow-citizen.

How often people reject Christ for materialistic reasons. One such person was my Chinese tailor in Saigon, Vietnam. Every time I visited his shop to have a suit made, every time he measured Donna, my wife, for a dress, we would give the man a gospel tract or invite him to the Chinese church a few blocks from his shop.

"Sorry, I'm too busy," was Mr. Wong's unvarying response. He was just too involved running his shop and making a living to search for the meaning of life.

But on April 30, 1975, South Vietnam fell to North Vietnam. Under the communists, Wong's business suffered, and after a few years he and his family fled to Hong Kong in a small fishing junk. By then I was pastoring an English-speaking church in Hong Kong.

Each week on my day off I visited the refugee camps. One particular day I saw someone waving at me from the great sea of faces in the camp. It was Wong! Making my way through the crowd, I welcomed my former tailor to Hong Kong. His first words to me were a question. "Where is your church?" he asked. "I want to go there!"

Sure enough, on Sunday he appeared at our church with his family. By the end of the morning he and his entire family had given their hearts to Christ! At a time when all his materialistic pursuits didn't matter and the real purpose of living had become clear, Wong came to Christ.

3. A great approach

As Jesus was getting into the boat, the man who had been demon-possessed begged to go with him. Jesus did not let him, but said, "Go home to your family and tell them how much the Lord has done for you, and how he has had mercy on you." So the man went away and began to tell in the Decapolis how much Jesus had done for him. And all the people were amazed. (Mark 5:18-20)

The miracles of Jesus most often became signposts pointing to His saving power. How beautifully this miracle led to a great evangelistic thrust in the 10 Cities. Having been delivered from Satan's bondage . . .

a. The formerly demented man wanted to follow Jesus.

The Gadarene may have wanted to follow Jesus for several reasons. He was most grateful to Jesus for delivering him from the demons. He must have admired a Man so powerful, so full of compassion. Perhaps also he was apprehensive about the demons. Now that the pigs were drowned, would the demons return to torment him? He may also have feared that his family and friends wouldn't accept him. And what about the owners of the pigs? Would they conclude that he was somehow responsible for their large financial loss and mistreat him?

Whatever his reasons, they melted under the Master's call. Jesus had a job for him to do right in his own community. So . . .

b. Jesus sent him back to his family.

His work was to be at home with his friends, relatives, associates and neighbors. He was to be a living letter for everyone to read. He was sane, not mad; holy, not unclean; gentle, not ferocious. Truly he was a "new creation; the old [had] gone, the new [had] come!" (2 Corinthians 5:17). His witness was to be among his old acquaintances where ofttimes it is most difficult to witness, but where our witness bears the most abundant and abiding fruit.

c. He shared with them his testimony.

I referred earlier in this chapter to Jeff. When Jeff's life changed, people in his network of relationships noticed the remarkable transformation. As a result he had abundant opportunities to share the gospel with them.

Jesus told the restored man from Gadara to go home and tell his family and friends what great things the Lord had done for him. John Soper suggests that his testimony may have gone something like this:

"You know what I was. You know what I am. Jesus made the difference. Are you interested?"

In an earlier chapter we addressed the power of personal testimony. Mark, a young man in our congregation, was a member of a local motorcycle group. He had been living a rather wild life when he came to Christ. Shortly afterward he took our evangelism training and developed a witnessing life-style. He led someone to Christ at work. It brought him so much joy that he started sharing the gospel with many people in the network of his relationships.

One day Mark went to get his long hair shortened. His barber noticed quite a change in Mark, and she started to ask questions. One thing led to another, and before long Mark was sharing his testimony and the gospel with her. In fact, his conversation became so extended that he was late for his EE class that night. Being late is a "no-no" in EE, so I asked Mark what had happened.

"I'm sorry, Pastor Tom," Mark apologized, his face reddening. "My hairdresser gave her heart to Christ this afternoon, and I had to stay a little longer for some immediate follow-up."

"Mark," I responded, "you can come late every week if you're leading others to Christ!"

The converted demoniac evidently shared his testimony because we're told that . . .

d. All the people in Decapolis were amazed.

Pay special attention to that comment because we are going to meet the people from Decapolis again! The testimony of the converted demoniac made an impact! His witness to his family and friends would not be forgotten! With that in mind, look at Mark 7:31-8:10 and take special note of this man's witness upon . . .

4. A great multitude

Then Jesus left the vicinity of Tyre and went through Sidon, down to the Sea of Galilee and into the region of the Decapolis. There some people brought to him a man who was deaf and could hardly talk, and they begged him to place his hand on the man.

After he took him aside, away from the crowd, Jesus put his fingers into the man's ears. Then he spit and touched the man's tongue. He looked up to heaven and with a deep sigh said to him, *"Ephphatha!"* (which means, "Be opened!"). At this, the man's ears were opened, his tongue was loosened and he began to speak plainly.

Jesus commanded them not to tell anyone. But the more he did so, the more they kept talking about it. People were overwhelmed with amazement. "He has done everything well," they said. "He even makes the deaf hear and the mute speak."

During those days another large crowd gathered. Since they had nothing to eat, Jesus called his disciples to him and said, "I have compassion for these people; they have already been with me three days and have nothing to eat. If I send them home hungry, they will collapse on the way, because some of them have come a long distance."

His disciples answered, "But where in this remote place can anyone get enough bread to feed them?"

"How may loaves do you have?" Jesus asked.

"Seven," they replied.

He told the crowd to sit down on the ground. When he had taken the seven loaves and given thanks, he broke them and gave them to his disciples to set before the people, and they did so. They had a few small fish as well; he gave thanks for them also and told the disciples to distribute them. The people ate and were satisfied. Afterward the disciples picked up seven basketfuls of broken pieces that were left over. About four thousand men were present. And having sent them away, he got into the boat with his disciples and went to the region of Dalmanutha. (Mark 7:31-8:10)

After some six weeks of ministry in Galilee that took Jesus as far northwest as Tyre and Sidon . . .

a. Jesus returned to the 10 Cities.

The restored demoniac had been testifying to his network of family, friends and neighbors. These people had seen the "before" picture. The evident change was impressive. They wanted to see and hear the Man Who had changed his life so radically. When word came that Jesus was again in their area, they poured out eagerly to meet Jesus. As a result, . . .

b. Jesus encountered a multitude.

As the crowd gathered, there were suffering people within the ranks. No doubt Jesus found all kinds of hurts to heal. That's the way to reach people: find a need and meet it; find a hurt and heal it!

In Omaha I became acquainted with Mark, a Jewish man who was facing a crisis in his life. He owned his own job placement business, but it was about to go bankrupt. He mentioned the fact to Ruth, a woman who worked in the same office building.

"I'm sure God is trying to tell you something," Ruth responded with concern.

"What do you think He's trying to tell me?" Mark asked.

"I don't know, but I know someone who does!" Ruth replied. She gave him my phone number. And not long after that I received a call from Mark, asking, "Pastor, what is God wanting to say to me?"

I offered to visit him in his home, but Mark vetoed the idea. His wife was a Catholic, and Mark wasn't sure she would let me in the house! So I invited Mark to my office. At the appointed hour he arrived. That evening he received Christ as his Savior. The danger of bankruptcy got Mark's attention and prepared him for the gospel of Christ.

c. Jesus healed a deaf mute.

The crowds increased in size. Great numbers of people followed Christ to see His miracles and listen to His teaching. So impressed were the people that they forgot to eat!

It is important to offer hurting people more than Bible verses or evangelistic outlines. God gave our church a burden to reach lost people in North Omaha. We had moved from the inner city and abandoned some of Omaha's neediest people.

After awhile God moved us to organize a ministry to the inner city. We called it COM-PASS Ministries. (COMPASS is an acronym for Christian Outreach to Multicultured People Assisting with Social Service.) We purchased a former bank building and called an experienced full-time director with vision for reaching the inner city. God is giving us a witness to a whole new segment of Omaha's population as we meet temporal and physical needs and share the gospel!

Jesus couldn't turn His back on the needs of the multitude when they were without food, so . . .

d. He fed 4,000 people.

Here we learn some very important lessons about how to reach people for Christ. We discover with John Soper a very basic approach. Let's call it . . .

5. A great principle

In the converted demoniac we see some important steps to reaching people for Christ:

a. The restored demoniac went back to his family and friends.

The newest Christian will always be the most effective evangelist. Usually we attribute this to the person's newfound zeal, and that's part of it. But the real reason they're most effective is because they have the largest network of non-Christian friends.

b. He did something Jesus couldn't do.

He could share Christ through his relationship of trust, through his network of friends, relatives, associates and neighbors. He needed Jesus for healing, but Jesus needed him and his network of relationships. So, if we are wise, we older Christians will help new Christians communicate the gospel to their spheres of influence. If we don't do that, they may go back home and discover rejection instead of open minds and hearts. So let's learn from the new convert and Jesus how . . .

c. He applied the "web of influence" principle.

If you will explore all the new believer's existing webs of influence, you will discover that more often than not there is at least one person who is ready to take the next step toward Christ.

In my own witnessing experiences, not all the people I've met on planes have responded to Christ. But there are the Noels and Tammys that were searching for God and a meaningful relationship with Him. Not all of my tennis friends have prayed to receive Christ, but Gordon did. Of all my neighbors whom I have sought to win to Christ, there is one family—Bill and Phyllis—whom God has brought to Himself.

The important thing is to persevere in praying, in building relationships, in seeking to share the gospel. Believe that there are people whom God will draw unto Himself!

d. The gospel always spreads best that way!

If you are an older Christian and over the years have been "lifted" out of non-Christian relationships, you will want to make new friends and build new webs of influence across which you can share the good news. You may want to explore natural bridges—anything about you which is similar to the non-Christians that you want to reach for Christ. Some of these things might be hobbies, interests, occupation and background.

Tom and I organized a Toastmasters Club at our church hoping to do two things: (1) help some of our leaders develop public-speaking skills and (2) bring some non-church people into our circle of friends. However, only one Catholic young man joined Tom and me. He suggested that we discontinue our threesome in favor of a similar club he attended at a nearby mall.

Unfortunately, my schedule didn't allow me to join the other group, but Tom joined. It turned out to be solidly Catholic. In fact, all the members were priests, nuns and lay Catholics. Tom didn't feel threatened, because he had come out of a Catholic background.

At one meeting it was decided that each participant should give an extemporaneous speech on the subject, "Why I chose the church I attend." One participant said he chose his church because it had plenty of parking space. The next said he chose his church because of the excellent air conditioning. A nun said she liked her church because they had comfortable kneelers.

When Tom's turn came he said that he had chosen his church because they introduced him to eternal life through Jesus Christ! And then he shared briefly exactly how a person could have eternal life and testified as to how he had trusted Christ. Tom had built a warm relationship with the club members. They asked if they could visit his church, so he arranged to give them a tour of the facility.

They were so impressed with Tom's life and testimony that they asked if he would share what he had said at a large meeting of local priests. The priests were so touched by what Tom said at their meeting that they arranged for him to speak to an even larger audience with the local Catholic bishop present! At that meeting Tom invited any who so wished to pray after him and then led in a salvation prayer. Then he asked anyone who had prayed to let him know. Two priests and a nun admitted that they had received Christ as their Savior. One of the priests declared that all his life he had been endeavoring to save himself through meritorious deeds!

What I've tried to illustrate here is that Tom reached out through a club to touch new people that were outside his church. He built a winsome relationship with them. Then God opened to him an opportunity to share Christ.

Whenever you encounter people in situations where you have little or nothing in common, you may want to consider building a special bridge. As I said earlier, find a need and meet it; find a hurt and heal it. That's what Jesus was constantly doing: healing the demoniac, the deaf mute and feeding the 4,000!

Lloyd was driving home from work one day when he encountered an auto accident. He pulled over to the curb and ran to the vehicle. He was glad to discover that, although her car had been totaled, the woman occupant was not injured. But how was she going to get home?

So Lloyd offered to wait until the police had filled out the accident report and then drive her home.

As they finally drove off from the accident

scene, Lloyd discovered that the woman lived 50 miles away! They hadn't gone very far before Lloyd's passenger exclaimed, "Lloyd, I could have been killed!"

What an opportunity! But Lloyd didn't respond with the gospel immediately. Rather, he waited until he had built a relationship and earned the right to share the gospel. Then he was ready to begin.

"Ma'am," Lloyd said, "suppose as you suggested a few minutes ago, you had been killed in that accident. Do you know for certain that you would have gone to heaven?" One thing led to another and the woman finally asked if they could pull over to the side of the road so she could pray to receive Christ as her Savior!

❈ ❈ ❈

At Pomona, New Jersey, Pastor John Soper followed the model he saw in Mark 5 and 7. He began applying the web of influence principle: having people focus their witness within their networks of relationships.

In 10 years 1,000 people came to Christ and seven "daughter" churches came into existence! This scriptural account in Mark's Gospel and church growth research both attest that the relational principle works!

Discussion Questions

1. Earlier in this book we noted that Jesus'

mission on earth was to seek and save the lost. Observing Satan at work in Mark 5:1-6, what would you say is *his* mission?

2. How have you observed Satan at work in society today? How might his defeat affect the illegitimate money-making motives and schemes in our society?

3. Why did the people in the 10 Cities region ask Jesus to leave their area? What changed that attitude so that multitudes flocked to Him?

4. How might the same spiritual dynamics be applied in our communities and society today?

5. What might you do and what might your church do to bring about a similar impact in the lives of non-Christians around you?

6. Discuss how the web of influence principle applies to the church and to individual Christians today.

7. What felt needs do your family, friends and neighbors evidence that you might meet?

Chapter Five

Developing
Meaningful Contacts

Mark 2:13-17

A S A COLLEGE STUDENT, C.T. Studd was a
star cricket player with a promising
career before him. He turned his back on it all
and sailed for Africa to serve God as a missionary. The compelling passion of his life
was to get out of his comfort zone to where
the action was—to get out of the four walls of
the church to where lost men and women
were dying in sin without any hope of abundant, eternal life. Such desire to develop
meaningful contacts with lost people moved
him to write:

Some want to live within the sound
  Of church or chapel bell;
I want to run a rescue shop
  Within a yard of hell!

The theme of this book is friendship evangelism. Specifically, I want to demonstrate how you can reach out redemptively to friends, relatives, associates and neighbors and effectively share Christ's saving gospel with them. I want to show you how you can build bridges to lost people even beyond your network of trust relationships and win them also to Christ.

Jesus was the perfect model of friendship evangelism. Better than anyone else, He knew how to get "out of the saltshaker" into the lost, needy society around Him. Note how Mark puts it:

> Once again Jesus went out beside the lake. A large crowd came to him, and he began to teach them. As he walked along, he saw Levi son of Alphaeus sitting at the tax collector's booth. "Follow me," Jesus told him, and Levi got up and followed him.
>
> While Jesus was having dinner at Levi's house, many tax collectors and "sinners" were eating with him and his disciples, for there were many who followed him. When the teachers of the law who were Pharisees saw

him eating with the "sinners" and tax
collectors, they asked his disciples:
"Why does he eat with tax collectors
and 'sinners'?"

On hearing this, Jesus said to them,
"It is not the healthy who need a doctor, but the sick. I have not come to
call the righteous, but sinners." (Mark
2:13-17)

The thesis of this chapter is simple: *Before you
can win people to Christ, you must establish mean-* /
ingful, friendly contact with them. In Mark's
description above, Jesus models for us four
very important steps that each of us must take
toward our non-Christian friends if we want to
win them to Christ. I call them salty contact, social contact, sinner contact and saving contact.
Jesus' first point of contact was what I have
labeled a . . .

1. Salty contact

In His sermon on the mount Jesus describes
His followers as "the salt of the earth" and "the
light of the world":

"You are the salt of the earth. But if
the salt loses its saltiness, how can it
be made salty again? It is no longer
good for anything, except to be
thrown out and trampled by men.

"You are the light of the world. A
city on a hill cannot be hidden.

Neither do people light a lamp and put it under a bowl. Instead they put it on its stand, and it gives light to everyone in the house. In the same way, let your light shine before men, that they may see your good deeds and praise your Father in heaven." (Matthew 5:13-16)

a. Christians are the salt of the earth.

After describing His followers as "the salt of the earth" and "the light of the world," Jesus warns them against losing their saltiness and hiding their light.

In what ways are we Christians to be like salt? We are to arrest the spread of corruption in society. We are to give spice and flavor to our society. How might we Christians lose our saltiness? In two ways. One, by failing to remain in Christ, the Source of our purifying, seasoning influence. Two, by limiting our influence to only church people. Probably the chief reason we Christians have so little influence on our world is a very simple one: we don't come in contact with the people we are supposed to salt!

Salt creates thirst. When non-Christians come in contact with you, you should make them thirsty for the Water of Life!

Jerry and Dottie are salty Christians who take their salt out of the "saltshaker" into the community and into their business. After I saw them bringing new people to our church on a regular basis, I sought them out.

"Jerry and Dottie," I asked, "what are you doing to impact so many people for Christ?"

"Oh, we're involved in network marketing," Jerry told me. "We make a lot of contacts by helping people make money and save money. We build relationships with our business associates. Then we invite them to our church's Easter or Christmas musicals. When they tell us they like what they've heard we invite them back to a regular Sunday service.

Quietly, graciously, unobtrusively, Jerry and Dottie—and others in their business—have been impacting people outside the four walls of our church and bringing them into the fellowship of God's people. That's another approach to friendship evangelism.

b. To be of any value, salt must get out of its shaker.

Christ did exactly that. He got out of the synagogue and into the community where lost sinners were. Notice that Christ "went out beside the lake. A large crowd came to him, and he began to teach them" (Mark 2:13). Increasingly Jesus took the gospel to those outside the synagogue. The open air became His church, the blue sky His canopy, the hillside or fishing boats His pulpit. Someone has aptly suggested that even as He was walking along a lakeside, Jesus was looking for opportunities. He was never off duty. If He could find one man like Levi, He reached out to him.

In his book, *Living Proof*, Jim Peterson states: "If we are going to engage the people of our generation, it will only happen on their turf." Oh, what a harvest we would gather if we like Jesus would look for opportunities to reach people out in the highways and byways of our work-a-day world!

c. Some Christians habitually avoid contact with unbelievers.

Notice how the Pharisees criticized Jesus for His contacts with "sinners." That was because they confined their daily contacts to people in the synagogue and to fellow orthodox Jews. Unfortunately, there are Christians who fall into the same exclusivism.

John Stott, speaking to a gathering of college and university students, calls such a person a "rabbit-hole Christian."

> [He] pops his head out of the hole, leaves his Christian roommate in the morning and scurries to class, only to frantically search for a Christian to sit next to. Thus he proceeds from class to class. When dinner time comes, he sits at one huge table with all the Christians in his dorm and thinks, 'What a witness!' From there he goes to his all-Christian Bible study. He

might even catch a prayer meeting where Christians pray for the non-believers on his floor. Then at night he scurries back to his Christian room-mate. Safe! He made it through the day and his only contacts with the world were those mad, brave dashes to and from Christian activities.

An overstatement, of course, but not without truth. Could you possibly have some of the same tendencies as you rush from Christian activity to Christian activity, passing by the very people with whom Christ wants you to have a salty contact?

d. We must see the needs of people outside the four walls of our church.

That is what the word *outreach* means. Having heard the gospel, having trusted Christ for eternal life, having heard the Word in Sunday school class and Sunday worship, God wants you to leave your "holy huddles" and reach out as a salty Christian in your neighborhood, at your place of employment, at the tennis club or on the golf course, among your unsaved family members, on the college campus and in every sphere of your daily activities.

As I write this chapter, I recall the Good Friday lunch conversation of a few weeks ago with a young man in our church whom I have been mentoring. Jim is a light bulb salesman and he started the conversation by saying the day before had been a bad one for sales.

"I lost my fourth best account," Jim admitted. "But this morning something very important happened! My wife Candy and I have been talking to Julie and her mom, who are our neighbors. Julie's brother is a lay pastor, but she doesn't know the Lord.

"Candy and I have been following your six-step graph for building relationships with Julie and her family. Our son Tyler has been dropping little bits of the gospel into our conversations with Julie and her son Rick. They've had a lot of questions which have helped us fill in the missing pieces of the gospel which they have needed.

"We had invited them to attend the Easter musical with us, so this morning I was talking with Julie about our plans to go together. She seemed so interested as we discussed Good Friday and Easter, that I finally asked her if she would like to receive the gift of eternal life. She said, 'Yes!' So we prayed together. Although yesterday I lost an important account, today I had the joy of leading Julie to Christ! What a week it's been!"

How exciting it is to see Christians getting out of the four walls of the sanctuary to reach their neighbors for Christ!

e. If sinners matter to us, we must develop more salty contacts with them.

And one of the best ways to do this is to follow Christ's example by reaching people through a . . .

2. Social contact

We saw from Mark's account that "Jesus was having dinner at Levi's house." Again, the word *house* is a form of the Greek word *oikos*. Jesus was doing exactly what He told the formerly demented man to do (see Chapter 4). He was taking the gospel to Levi's friends, relatives, associates and neighbors.

a. We need to develop social contact with our work associates away from the job.

Mark refers particularly to "many tax collectors." Levi had spent much time working with those people. He had earned their friendship and maybe even their trust through years of association in the same occupation with them. After Levi yielded himself to Christ, he wished for his friends to share his great discovery. So he invited Christ and all of his friends from work to a big house party. Jesus would be the Guest of honor.

b. Homes are great places in which to develop social contact.

One of the best ways to develop social contact with non-Christians is to invite them to your home for a dessert or a meal. It can be a barbecue, some homemade ice cream, a potluck or a birthday party. As a general rule have a definite reason for inviting them. It may be just to see a video of your recent vacation trip or to try your new recipe for fixing the fish you caught. Don't be too elaborate with crystal, china and sterling silver. Guests probably will be more relaxed with something barbecued and a Coke. If you are too fancy your friends will be less likely to reciprocate.

c. If you find it difficult to entertain in your home, invite a friend from church gifted in hospitality to help you.

Question: Who did Levi invite to help him entertain his friends from work? Jesus, the master Host! How might a friend help you? By preparing and serving food. By helping with the conversation. By sharing his or her testimony if the opportunity presents itself.

Explain your problem to your Christian friends and blend their gifts of entertaining with your concern for your lost friends. Don't feel compelled to say something "spiritual" but use the opportunity to show forth the love of Christ. Since it is your home, feel free to have grace at the meal. In your prayer be brief, but thank the Lord by name for your neighbors present. Don't preach or try to share a quick witness.

If one of the neighbors brings a bottle of wine as a gesture of friendship, don't panic. Respond in a loving, sensitive manner. Remember that this is a socially accepted grace in the non-

Christian community.

This coming Christmas we are planning to organize a number of Christmas coffees throughout the city in the homes of our church folk. We will be training our people how to invite their neighbors over for coffee and refreshments. Each one present will share what Christmas means to him or her. At each home a designated couple will, in addition, weave the gospel into their remarks. We're hoping that this will lead to many of our congregation's friends and neighbors coming to Christ. We hope that many of them will also attend our church's Christmas musical where again the message of salvation will be presented.

One of the most effective witnesses that I experienced while pastoring in Hong Kong was also at Christmas. Every year our church rented a banquet room at the Holiday Inn. Then we asked each of our church people to reserve a table or two for their friends, neighbors and family members. We began the evening with several secular songs and skits including a visit from Santa. Then we presented sacred Christmas music and a Christmas message. It was a low-key approach that built bridges of friendship with many non-Christians and prepared the way for a more direct witness. As a result a good number of the congregation's friends and families came to Christ.

Sometimes it is difficult to bring friends to your home for a meal. How about inviting them to a neutral place? For a number of years we organized what we called a "Fall Spectacular." Our first speaker was Josh McDowell. For four days and nights we organized various breakfasts, luncheons and dinners to which our church people could invite their friends. Hundreds of non-Christians came to hear Josh. Many of them trusted Christ. The next year we invited astronaut Jim Irwin and the following year Adolph Coors. Football great, Jeff Siemon, of the Vikings was another speaker. Charlie ("Tremendous") Jones was still another.

With a little creative planning, the church can provide such opportunities for building bridges and helping people take their salty witness out into the community.

d. Look for common interests about which to converse.

Sports, hobbies, vacation spots, cars, clothes, family members and their favorite pastimes are some of the subjects most people are comfortable discussing. Above all be a good listener. Keep the get-together "you"-focused. That is, be sure to take a great interest in your guests' interests.

The next time your church has a "FRANtastic Sunday"—remember the acronym: *f*riends, *r*elatives, *a*ssociates, *n*eighbors—you and your family might want to consider inviting some of your "FRAN" to the Sunday morning service followed afterward by a cookout at your house!

Social contacts such as this will help provide

your need for a meaningful . . .

3. Sinner contact

God expects you to make contact with non-Christians. Jesus attended Levi's dinner party for that express purpose.

a. You must deliberately penetrate the non-Christian world outside of your church.

Mark notes specifically that "many tax collectors and 'sinners' were eating with him and his disciples." In Christ's day and culture this was quite a controversial thing to do. In fact, the religious leaders criticized Him. "Why does he eat with tax collectors and 'sinners'?"

Question: In our day and culture, could this still be a controversial step for a Christian to take? Some separatist, legalistic churchgoers might question your motives and even accuse you of "worldliness."

b. Sinner contact can begin with only one person.

Jesus's sinner contact began with Levi, whom He found sitting in a tax collector's booth probably made of branches erected at the entrance into the town. In calling Levi to follow Him (Mark 2:14), our Lord called a most unlikely candidate—a member of a trade considered to be of very dubious merit.

Levi the publican dealt with public money. The Roman government had devised a tax collection system that operated at maximum efficiency and minimum cost to the government. Rome *auctioned* the right to collect taxes in certain areas. The person who bought that right was responsible to the Roman government for an agreed sum. Anything he could raise over and above that figure he was allowed to keep as commission.

Obviously, the system lent itself to grave abuses. In an era of no newspapers, radio or television, people did not know how much they ought to pay. Nor had they any right of appeal. The consequence was that many tax collectors became wealthy through illegal extortion.

Not surprisingly, these tax collectors, being notoriously dishonest, were universally hated. Not only did they fleece their own countrymen, but they also did their best to swindle the government. By Jewish law a tax collector was barred from the synagogue. He was ranked among the unclean beasts. Tax collectors, robbers and murderers were classed together.

c. New believers have many non-Christian contacts.

If you want to make contact with sinners, get in touch with someone who recently has come to Christ. Many tax collectors and sinners came to Levi's house for dinner. They knew him well, and he knew them. They felt comfortable in his home. Apparently they trusted him.

In his book *Lifestyle Evangelism*, Joseph Aldrich

tells us that the average new Christian for the first two years of his conversion has significant relationships with non-Christians. But his conversion opens up a whole new web of relationships with Christians. Hence he inadvertently drifts away from his non-Christian associates.

What has been *your* experience since coming to Christ? Do you have more or fewer non-Christian friends? Why?

d. One new-believer friend may serve as a bridge to reach other non-Christians.

It is interesting to note that not only did Jesus call Levi, a person of such infamy, to be His follower (we know him more commonly as Matthew, an apostle and the writer of the first Gospel), but Jesus used His relationship with Levi as a bridge to reach others of his trade and sinful background. Jesus accepted an invitation to Levi's home for dinner with a whole crowd of bad characters with the same questionable occupation. He didn't simply show Himself as kindly disposed towards such sinners. He associated with them!

You too will do well to capitalize on the new-believer's network of non-Christian friends and help him or her reach them for Christ as early after his or her conversion as possible.

e. Contact with sinners should never lead to compromise.

I had the joy of leading Carol, a church

visitor, to Christ and seeing her grow in Christ. Later she became my daughter-in-law. Carol enrolled in our evangelism training and began to reach out to her unsaved family members and work associates.

Carol began witnessing to Joanna at her Tupperware office. Joanna was full of questions and was truly searching. Having seen the beauty of Christ in Carol's life, she wanted to visit our church. She came with her husband a few times but didn't seem to make the "plunge" into trusting Christ.

Finally, Carol asked if I would visit Joanna and Dan in their home to see if I might be able to bring them to a place of commitment. It wasn't difficult. Carol's life and witness had left a convincing impact! Serving in the reserves, Dan was called into active duty and was sent off to fight in the Middle East. When he returned he continued to be active in our church until Joanna and Dan had a job transfer to another state.

Though Jesus ate with sinners, He nevertheless maintained His purity. Of course, we too must be careful to avoid compromise. While we mix with sinners and seek to influence them for Christ, we are to remain separated from sin, remembering that Jesus prayed to God the Father, "My prayer is not that you take them out of the world but that you protect them from the evil one" (John 17:15).

Christ found the right balance. He exerted an

effective impact because of His identification with our sinful race. But in the midst of that identification He maintained a pure testimony by distancing Himself from humanity's sinful ways. His sinner contact was for the purpose of communicating His love and His saving truth. And never once did He mar that communication by compromise or contamination!

Having come to Christ, you, like Jesus, are to penetrate human society. You are to mix with unbelievers. You are to try to think in their patterns, to listen to their questions, to understand their worldview. You are to feel their burdens and to respond to their needs.

But that is not enough! You must go one step further to establish with them . . .

4. Saving contact

Jesus said, "I have not come to call the righteous, but sinners." He did not come into this world just to be with sinners. He came to seek and to save sinners! But how did He—and how must you—establish saving contact with them?

a. Believe strongly in the saving power of the gospel.

Another question: The fishermen disciples—Peter, James, John and Andrew—for years may have paid inflated taxes to Matthew. How do you think they would have felt about Jesus' calling their swindling tax collector to follow Him? Answer: Surprised!

The other disciples probably had serious doubts about Levi's qualifications. Why then do you suppose Jesus chose him? Jesus saw Levi's potential as a trophy of divine grace and transforming power.

In this short account we have unquestionably one of the greatest instances in the New Testament of Jesus' power to see in a person, not only what he was but also what he could be! He saw in this low-down, despised, publican the potential to become an apostle! He saw in this crooked sinner who used his pen to cheat people out of their money the potential to become a Spirit-inspired author of the good news. Jesus, being God, knew what God could do.

You too must believe that the gospel has power to transform your non-Christian friends, relatives and business associates.

b. Expect to be criticized.

By keeping company with publicans and tax collectors Jesus was doing something which the pious people of His day would never have done. Orthodox Jews were forbidden to go on a journey with publicans, to do any business with them, to give anything to them, to receive anything from them, to entertain them as guests or to be guests in their homes.

Because of His contact with sinners, Christ was misunderstood and maligned by the religious people of His day. He outraged their prejudices and violated the accepted rules of their religious society.

As you develop sinner contacts for redemptive purposes, you also risk being misunderstood. All too often fellow believers will misapply biblical teaching on separation. Too frequently they will view sinners as enemies rather than friends, forgetting that Jesus was called a "Friend of sinners."

c. Go where the need is.

When criticized for His actions, Jesus simply responded that He was going where the need was the greatest! He reminded His critics that He would be a poor Doctor if He visited only houses where people enjoyed good health. His task was to go to the ill who really needed Him!

What a contrast with the Pharisees who were more concerned with preserving their own holiness. They were more like doctors who would diagnose disease but offer no cure, lest they should be infected. Essentially they were selfish—more concerned with saving themselves than bringing salvation to others.

d. Seek out unbelievers, enjoy dinner with them, talk to them and when the opportune time comes, offer them Christ's saving grace.

Human need was what drew Jesus. He came to call sinners to repentance. Therefore He sought out sinners, ate with them, conversed with them and shared with them the good news of His marvelous salvation. His perfect purity could not be soiled by their companionship; rather He brought to them cleansing for their sins. He had come, after all, to seek and to *save* that which was lost!

Hence He commanded His disciples to do the same. And He encourages you today in like manner. There is no heart so vile that the Lord will not enter when invited (Revelation 3:20). There is no sinner so low that Jesus cannot save him or her (Psalm 40:1-3; 2 Corinthians 5:17).

But will you inconvenience yourself to offer saving contact to those within the network of your relationships? Or will you play it safe and stay within the comfort zone of your Christian friends and church?

Joseph Aldrich says that the best argument for Christianity is Christians who are rubbing shoulders with non-Christians, allowing the beauty of the indwelling Christ to be lived out in their everyday relationships. The most convincing evidence for Christianity is the Christian's joy, certainty, completeness. When these are cultivated and communicated, evangelism is the glorious result. Thus we might conclude that . . .

e. Saving contact means opening the web of your relationships to include nonbelievers and allowing Jesus' beauty and saving truth to be communicated through you.

Saving contact is expressing what you possess in Christ and then, when God gives you the opportunity, explaining how you came to possess it. Stated concisely, it is both visualization and verbalization of the gospel.

How much effort are you putting forth to build bridges with non-Christians? Going out of your way to make friends is absolutely crucial if you want to reach them for Christ.

One day in Hong Kong I went to a leather goods store to shop for a briefcase and a new belt. In passing, I told the shop's owner, Henry Lai, that I had bought my old belt and wallet in Vietnam.

He responded that he had spent a short time with a Chinese business firm in Saigon. When he learned that I was a pastor, he told me that he was planning to get married soon and wondered if he could use our church. Since the English-speaking Chinese church I was pastoring only allowed members to be married there, I told him that it would be impossible. But I told him that Donna and I would very much like to attend his wedding wherever it was held. Henry and his bride were married by the justice of the peace. Donna and I attended.

As they left for their honeymoon, the groom and bride said they wanted to visit our church when they returned, because they didn't have a church home. Sure enough, when they returned they started attending. And it wasn't too long before both of them received Christ and became members of our church!

They wanted to know how I had learned to

share the gospel so clearly. I told them that a pastor in America named D. James Kennedy had a big part in training me. They were so grateful that they named their first baby James! And it all started while talking about some leather goods and our mutual experiences in Vietnam.

Are you praying for those within your *oikos*? Will you reach out to those who are unbelievers? Will you allow Jesus to help you impact them with the good news? Will you develop with your friends, relatives, associates and neighbors salty, social, sinner-saving contacts?

Can you effectively present the gospel to these people when the opportunity is there? Can you bring them to a place of commitment? If you cannot effectively present the gospel and bring a person to a place of commitment, will you prayerfully consider enrolling in Evangelism Explosion training at your church? If your church doesn't offer the training, start praying that God will move your pastor and church leaders to bring the training to your church.

Discussion Questions

1. What are some of the functions of salt? How in practical terms can you as a Christian be used as salt in your community?

2. What is your church doing to encourage and equip its members to get out of the "saltshaker"?

3. What are some of the good Christian or church activities that might be causing us to resemble—as John Stott calls them—"rabbit-hole Christians"?

4. List and discuss some innovative approaches that you might try in your home to build bridges with your unbelieving friends, neighbors and work associates.

5. What are some other social contacts that you might develop or the church might plan to help you reach people outside the church?

6. What are some of the dangers you might encounter while seeking to identify with non-Christians? How might you maintain a consistent noncompromising testimony while at the same time socializing with non-Christians?

7. Does your church offer Evangelism Explosion training? If it does not, what steps would be required to incorporate the training? If it does, have you taken the course?

Chapter Six

Capitalizing on People's Openness

Acts 16:6-34

DENISE'S GRANDMOTHER was taken to the hospital with a serious illness. Because she was over 90, it was uncertain whether she would ever return home. Denise and her husband Tom shared the gospel with the elderly woman, but because they were so relatively young, she didn't take their witness seriously.

Since Denise's grandmother had profound respect for clergymen, Denise asked if I would visit her and share the gospel with her. But I had a better idea. I asked Annie, who was a little older than Tom and Denise, to go with me to the hospital and stay with the grandmother all afternoon until an opportunity presented itself for witness.

At last the opening came. Annie patiently, lovingly explained the plan of salvation and the grandmother prayed to invite Christ into her heart as Savior and Lord. The elderly woman was elated, but she had one problem. She had been searching for eternal life for a long time. Why did she have to wait for so long to hear such wonderful news?

Knowing that people are searching for God will greatly motivate you to witness to them. All around you there are spiritually receptive people. From Paul's very successful ministry at Philippi, I want to set forth five basic principles to help you understand and handle the evangelistic receptivity right in your community.

1. Openness

The resurrected Christ is declared to be the One "who holds the key of David. What he opens no one can shut, and what he shuts no one can open" (Revelation 3:7). From Acts 16, notice some ways in which He does a little of both. First . . .

a. Jesus closes some doors.

Paul and his companions traveled throughout the region of Phrygia and Galatia, having been kept by the Holy Spirit from preaching the word in the

> province of Asia. When they came to
> the border of Mysia, they tried to
> enter Bithynia, but the Spirit of Jesus
> would not allow them to. So they
> passed by Mysia and went down to
> Troas. (16:6-8)

Paul must have thought it strange that the
Spirit of Jesus should close the door to the
Roman province of Asia, even temporarily. Evidently the harvest there wasn't quite ripe. How
do you think the Holy Spirit communicated
with Paul? William Barclay suggests that it may
have been by some physical infirmity that Paul
later refers to as his "thorn in the flesh." This
explanation Barclay draws from verse 10 where
there emerge a series of "we" references indicat-
ing that Luke, the human author of Acts and a
medical doctor, had joined the missionary team.
Luke may have felt that Paul's physical problem demanded a change of course.

God frequently uses circumstances to cut us
off from persons with whom we might have intended to share the gospel or whom we long to
lead to Christ. It may have been the person's
apparent rebuff of our attempts to reach out to
him, or it may be because of some handicap or
limitation on our part. In such uncontrollable
situations, we must bow to God's sovereign
timing and perfect process. But while we may
be grieved over God's closing of some doors,
we can rejoice that . . .

b. God opens other doors.

> During the night Paul had a vision of
> a man of Macedonia standing and
> begging him, "Come over to
> Macedonia and help us." After Paul
> had seen the vision, we got ready at
> once to leave for Macedonia, conclud-
> ing that God had called us to preach
> the gospel to them. (16:9-10)

Evidently God knew that the people of
Macedonia were much more ready for the
gospel. The fruit was ripe. The fish were biting.
It was a little bit like the time in John 21 when
Peter at his Lord's bidding after a night of
empty toil let down his net on the other side of
the boat and pulled in so many fish that the net
broke and the ship almost sank. Just as our
Lord knows where the fish are in the sea, so He
can ably direct you to responsive places. He
gave Paul a vision that redirected his steps
toward a more responsive open door in
Macedonia. And that turned out to be one of
the most fruitful places of Paul's entire ministry.

c. Spiritually, God opens hearts.

> On the Sabbath we went outside the
> city gate to the river, where we ex-
> pected to find a place of prayer. We

sat down and began to speak to the women who had gathered there. One of those listening was a woman named Lydia, a dealer in purple cloth from the city of Thyatira, who was a worshiper of God. The Lord opened her heart to respond to Paul's message. (16:13-14)

By His Spirit, God lays His hand upon us and touches the deepest springs of our nature. Sometimes He does it by causing us to become dissatisfied with the physical and temporal things that surround us, drawing our thoughts upward and higher to eternal and spiritual matters. Much like the flower is opened by the warm rays of the sun, so our calloused hearts and closed minds are softened and opened by God's love and grace.

Other times God employs various circumstances to warn, to woo and to win our hearts, so that we might pay close attention to His saving truth. Exactly how He did it with Lydia we are not told, but it is evident that something supernatural prepared the way for Paul's loving witness. And the same thing happens in our day. How else can we explain why sometimes we present the gospel and it seems to fall on deaf ears, while on other occasions we share the same basic message and it finds an enthusiastic, believing response?

I was born in central Vietnam's imperial capital, Hue. My parents labored there as missionaries for many years. Because Hue was where the emperor lived and reigned and because it was a strong seat of Buddhism, its residents were very resistant to the gospel. You might say their minds were almost closed to the gospel.

On the main street of Hue, Mr. Ngo cang Ngo owned and operated a gas station where my dad often bought gas. His station was across the street from Mr. Thanh Tin's watch and jewelry shop. Frequently Mr. Thanh shared the gospel with Mr. Ngo, but God's truth seemed to fall on deaf ears.

Many times Mr. Ngo visited our church. He heard my dad's sermons, listened to my mother play the pump organ and my brothers and sisters play their musical instruments. But for some 40 years Mr. Ngo gave no thought to receiving Christ as his Savior.

In 1976, a little more than a year after communist armies from the north conquered South Vietnam, Ngo escaped by boat to Hong Kong. One day in a refugee camp in Hong Kong, he heard me preach the gospel and came forward to receive Christ as his Savior. His whole family believed with him. Today he lives in San Diego, California, and attends our Vietnamese Alliance church there. How wonderful it was to see God open the door to his heart, which for so many years had been closed tightly!

d. Satan closes minds.

> Once when we were going to the place of prayer, we were met by a slave girl who had a spirit by which she predicted the future. She earned a great deal of money for her owners by fortune-telling. This girl followed Paul and the rest of us, shouting, "These men are servants of the Most High God, who are telling you the way to be saved." (16:16-17)

Clearly, Satan was at work in the mind of the slave girl, confusing, binding and blinding her so that she would not turn to Christ. The girl, in fact, became Satan's instrument to turn others away from the Savior.

In our day Satan is still the great adversary of the gospel. Jesus says Satan is the one who takes away the seed of God's Word when it has been planted in people's hearts (Mark 4:15). He darkens the minds of the unbelieving to prevent them from seeing the light of the gospel. Christians need to be aware of Satan's activity among unbelievers.

e. God sends crises.

> Suddenly there was such a violent earthquake that the foundations of the prison were shaken. At once all the

prison doors flew open, and everybody's chains came loose. The jailer woke up, and when he saw the prison doors open, he drew his sword and was about to kill himself because he thought the prisoners had escaped. But Paul shouted, "Don't harm yourself! We are all here!"

The jailer called for lights, rushed in and fell trembling before Paul and Silas. He then brought them out and asked, "Sirs, what must I do to be saved?" (16:26-30)

While God often opens hearts by the still, small voice of His Spirit, sometimes He has to take more drastic steps to capture people's attention. In this situation, it took an earthquake to awaken the Philippian jailer to his spiritual need.

In his book, *Seasons of Life*, Charles Swindoll shares an incident that took place in 1968 on an airliner bound for New York. As the plane made its approach to the airport, the pilot realized the landing gear was not engaging. Crew members tried manually to lock it in place, without success. Responding to the crisis, airport personnel sprayed the runway with foam as fire trucks and other emergency vehicles moved into position. Passengers were told to place their heads between their knees and grab their ankles just before impact.

Suddenly the pilot announced over the intercom: "We are beginning our final descent. At this moment, in accordance with international aviation codes established in Geneva, it is my obligation to inform you that if you believe in God, you should commence to pray."

Swindoll goes on to remark how amazing it is that society has to be pushed to the brink, when all escape routes are closed, before it recognizes that God just might be there and that "you should commence to pray."

Mike, after 30 years of rebellion against God, gave his life over to Jesus Christ. What caused the dramatic change? Five weeks earlier he began feeling sick. He became convinced that something terrible was wrong with him. He concluded that he was going to die. After almost losing his mind from worry, Mike prayed to God for help. For the first time he felt that God had answered his prayer. Something changed inside him. Mike began to search for God's truth. He found eternal life in Christ and has evidenced genuine spiritual growth.

As one of Christ's witnesses, you need to be alert to the crises God brings into people's lives. You need to realize that by this means He may be preparing their hearts for the truth of His gospel. At times like that, may God help you to respond in true . . .

2. Obedience

From the Acts passage, it is clear that just as God is preparing people's hearts to receive a gospel witness, He is also calling and sending forth His people to witness.

a. God's call

> After Paul had seen the vision, we got ready at once to leave for Macedonia, concluding that God had called us to preach the gospel to them. (Acts 16:10)

Most Christians when hearing references to a "call" think of that somewhat mysterious divine summons to full-time pastoral or missionary service. But Paul had already received such a call on the road to Damascus (see Acts 9:15-17). What then was this "call"? Clearly God was directing Paul to a new evangelistic target on the continent of Europe. But how does God communicate His call in situations like that? Well . . .

b. To some God gives a vision.

> During the night Paul had a vision of a man of Macedonia standing and begging him, "Come over to Macedonia and help us." After Paul had seen the vision, we got ready at once to leave for Macedonia, concluding that God had called us to preach the gospel to them. (16:9-10)

In our day, too, God gives some Christians a deep, compelling conviction concerning the place He wants them to go or the thing He wants them to do. He gave such a vision to William Cameron Townsend, founder of Wycliffe Bible Translators, to translate the Bible into the many remaining languages of the world. But whether or not you have heard a call or seen a vision, it is important for you to realize that . . .

c. To all believers God gives a command.

Christ commanded, "Go and make disciples of all nations" (Matthew 28:19). It is a commission to every Christian. Jesus has commanded every Christian to witness and make disciples.

What will be your response? If you follow Paul's example, you will comply promptly and wholeheartedly. "After Paul had seen the vision, we got ready at once to leave for Macedonia, concluding that God had called us to preach the gospel to them" (16:10). Paul didn't "let any grass grow under his feet!" He didn't procrastinate. He didn't make some nice-sounding promises. He got going. And if you have not done so yet, you need to get going, too.

One of the most important concerns in personal evangelism is the element of time. Every Christian must "redeem the time." He or she must lay hold of the opportunities God presents. "Now is the day of salvation." (2 Corinthians 6:2). Tomorrow may be too late!

Once every six weeks, Tom sold wholesale

toys, school supplies and assorted gifts in Belleville, Kansas. On one such trip, the owner of an appliance store recommended that Tom try lunching at a certain restaurant on the edge of town. The place was packed, but Tom found one empty booth and sat there. Presently, an older man walked up and asked if he might share the booth.

As Tom and John got acquainted, Tom discovered that the 62-year-old semi-retired farmer ate lunch there every day. As they talked, John admitted that farming had its "ups and downs." It gave him no peace of mind. Although Tom was very busy, he asked the farmer's permission to share with him how, through the gospel, he had found deep peace in this life and eternal life for the world to come. He finished by inviting John to receive Christ into his life. The farmer did so with great joy and sincerity.

Tom gave him some literature and promised to visit him upon returning to Belleville six weeks later.

"You can find me here at this restaurant every noon!" John assured him.

When Tom returned, there was John! Only this time he had a new joy in his life that was obvious. He had finished reading the Gospel of John and was reading other books of the Bible. Tom encouraged him to attend church and promised to meet him in another six weeks.

Because Christmas was approaching, Tom remained in Kansas selling gifts for three more days. So excited was he about John's rapid growth in Christ that he decided to stop at Belleville for lunch on his way home. This time John wasn't at the restaurant. "John won't be eating here anymore," one of the waitresses explained sadly. "His family buried him this morning."

Tom, of course, was shocked by the news, but he rejoiced that he, like the Apostle Paul, had been prompt in his . . .

d. Proclamation of good news

> After Paul had seen the vision, we got ready at once to leave for Macedonia, concluding that God had called us to preach the gospel to them. (16:10)

That phrase "preach the gospel" may be a misleading translation of the Greek. Some Christians believe only ordained pastors or missionaries can legitimately "preach the gospel." But in the original Greek, the phrase simply means "proclaim or announce good news." That is something every Christian—old or young, seasoned or new—can and should do. If you do not pass on the wonderful news of life to your friends, relatives, associates and neighbors, who will? They are your responsibility. They are your evangelistic field!

One of the obstacles that keeps many from

witnessing is the misconception that non-Christians just aren't interested. But if you knew all the facts, you would be surprised at how many people around you are sincerely searching for the truth and for eternal life.

When three students from Burke High School in Omaha were tragically killed in a car accident, the youth throughout our city became very thoughtful about death.

One of our church high schoolers, Sam, invited a classmate named Adam to an all-night youth social at the church. The event is organized to be a fun time but also to give our Christian youth an evangelistic outreach to their friends. Every hour the youth go to a different place in the city to do something fun like miniature golf, bowling, swimming, skating. As they ride in the bus between places or stand around enjoying refreshments, the Christian youth have time to approach their non-Christian friends with their personal testimony and the gospel.

A few weeks after the all-nighter Mark, Jessica and Sheryl visited Adam to see what he thought of it. "Oh, I'm searching for something," Adam responded. Another one of our youth had shared the gospel with him when he was a freshman, and he expected—actually hoped—that Mark, Jessica and Sheryl would give him something to fill the vacuum in his life.

Since the deaths of the three students were still fresh in everyone's mind, Mark used the incident to lead into the gospel. Adam said he didn't go to the funeral because funerals are sad and he was afraid of death. Mark told him that Christ could take away that fear and replace it with an assurance of eternal life. Adam was so open that he prayed right then and there to invite Christ into his life.

e. Prayer for God's direction

> On the Sabbath we went outside the city gate to the river, where we expected to find a place of prayer. We sat down and began to speak to the women who had gathered there. (16:13)

It is evident from the above verse that Paul was a man of prayer. He met with people who prayed and, no doubt, prayed much in private. It is important that you pray for people whom you want to see come to Christ, especially for direction as to how and when to proceed. Ask God to arrange divine appointments for you each day.

3. Opposition

One of the most certain facts of personal evangelism is that you will always encounter opposition. Whenever you are reaching out to people with good news about eternal life, you can expect an all-out attack from Satan on every front.

a. Satan hates the gospel.

Satan hates anything to do with God, the gospel, the church and Christians. Being the enemy of our souls and the father of lies, he seeks to blind people's eyes to God's truth, bind their wills and pluck away the seed of the gospel when it is sown in their hearts. Therefore you must be alert. The Scriptures say . . .

b. Satan is an angel of light and can be defeated.

> Once when we were going to the place of prayer, we were met by a slave girl who had a spirit by which she predicted the future. She earned a great deal of money for her owners by fortune-telling. This girl followed Paul and the rest of us, shouting, "These men are servants of the Most High God, who are telling you the way to be saved." She kept this up for many days. Finally Paul became so troubled that he turned around and said to the spirit, "In the name of Jesus Christ I command you to come out of her!" At that moment the spirit left her. (16:16-18)

Look how Satan deceived a slave girl in Philippi and through her was seeking to deceive many others interested in the truth. He appeared to promote evangelism, but in actuality he was undermining it.

In addition to satanic opposition, . . .

c. We must also expect vehement opposition from people.

Jesus once commented that "men loved darkness instead of light because their deeds were evil" (John 3:19). So you must remember that if someone turns a deaf ear to the gospel, he rejects God, not you!

> When the owners of the slave girl realized that their hope of making money was gone, they seized Paul and Silas and dragged them into the marketplace to face the authorities. They brought them before the magistrates and said, "These men are Jews, and are throwing our city into an uproar by advocating customs unlawful for us Romans to accept or practice."
> The crowd joined in the attack against Paul and Silas, and the magistrates ordered them to be stripped and beaten. After they had been severely flogged, they were thrown into prison, and the jailer was commanded to guard them carefully. Upon receiving such orders, he put them in the inner cell and fastened

their feet in the stocks. (16:19-24)

No one enjoys rejection or being rebuffed for the gospel. What makes it extra painful is the fact that you are reaching out to people with love, that you have a message that can change their lives and that you have the answer to their hearts' needs. You need to remember that sinners rejected the Savior. They rebuffed Paul and threw him in prison for telling them the truth. Knowing that they are rejecting God rather than you will reduce the tension and help you to persevere in love. Ofttimes the person who opposes the gospel may not realize that . . .

d. People's wrath promotes God's purposes.

About midnight Paul and Silas were praying and singing hymns to God, and the other prisoners were listening to them. (16:25)

In his difficulty, the psalmist says to God, "Surely your wrath against men brings you praise" (Psalm 76:10). See how Paul and Silas responded to opposition with praise to God for His sovereign wisdom. This, in turn, led to an opportunity to share the gospel with their fellow inmates and the jailer. Notice how beautifully the hearts of Paul and Silas . . .

4. Overflow

Overflowing is what evangelism really is

about! In fact, biblical evangelism is not a special activity assigned at a prescribed time, but the constant and spontaneous *overflow* of a believer's individual and corporate experiences and knowledge of Christ. But, of course, if it is going to overflow . . .

a. The heart must first be filled.

> About midnight Paul and Silas were praying and singing hymns to God, and the other prisoners were listening to them. (16:25)

The heart must be filled with God's grace and truth, but above all filled by the Holy Spirit. Only persons filled with the Holy Spirit can praise God in situations such as the one that faced Paul and Silas. No one is a better advertisement for the gospel than the person who is filled with joy and praise.

As I mentioned earlier, I do quite a bit of mentoring at our church. Bryan graduated from Moody Bible Institute in Chicago and was headed for missionary service in Russia. But his mission board felt he needed some experience in a U.S. church before going overseas. They contacted me and I agreed to mentor Bryan for one year.

Among other items there are three ministries that all of my interns are required to become involved in: (1) a regular outreach prayer meeting held early every Saturday morning, (2) Masterplanning training for leadership and (3) Evangelism Explosion (EE) training.

Bryan had not completed his first semester of EE training when he realized that biblical evangelism, as we understand it, is not a special activity that we engage in at an assigned time but the spontaneous overflow of a Spirit-filled, Spirit-equipped Christian. It begins with a Christ-like life and walk and leads to a loving verbal witness in God's perfect timing.

I like for my interns to have part-time secular jobs so they can have "salty" contact with non-Christians. Bryan therefore obtained an assistant manager position with a local McDonald's. His boss and fellow employees watched his life carefully. They knew he intended to be a missionary and even jokingly remarked that the big golden *M* in front of their workplace stood for "Missionary Bryan"!

Having watched his consistent life-style, they began to listen to his words. One particular fellow employee met regularly with Bryan for coffee breaks and started asking questions about the gospel. After an extended time of sharing—about three months—the young man confessed Christ as Savior.

Do your friends and neighbors see an inexplicable joy in you? Do you exhibit this kind of overflow from your life each day? But more than this . . .

b. The person who would win people to Christ must be ready.

Whether entering into a conversation with a group of women on a river bank or by sharing the gospel with a Roman jailer in the middle of the night, Paul and Silas were ready! They were ready first of all with a consistent lifestyle.

> But Paul shouted, "Don't harm yourself! We are all here!"
> The jailer called for lights, rushed in and fell trembling before Paul and Silas. (16:28-29)

Paul and Silas were submitting to the authorities instead of running through the open prison doors. But they were also ready with a saving message.

> [The jailer] then brought them out and asked, "Sirs, what must I do to be saved?"
> They replied, "Believe in the Lord Jesus, and you will be saved—you and your household." Then they spoke the word of the Lord to him and to all the others in his house. (16:30-32)

The greatest cry of the human heart is, "What must I do to be saved?" And the greatest reply you can give is simply, "Believe in the Lord Jesus Christ, and you will be saved."

Shortly after Wayne's 747 flight touched down in Tokyo, the pilot announced that there was a report of a bomb having been placed on the plane. After a careful search, however, the report was concluded to be a false alarm. On the next flight, after most of the passengers had fallen asleep, Wayne walked around the cabin. One of the flight attendants, Linda, approached Wayne to see if something was wrong.

Wayne responded that he couldn't sleep on planes. She asked him what he liked to do.

"I like to talk to people," Wayne responded. So Linda invited Wayne to talk to her. When she learned that he had been on the plane with the bomb scare, she inquired why he wasn't afraid. Wayne assured her that it was because he knew he had eternal life. Since Linda didn't have that assurance, Wayne asked her if he could share with her how she could discover that same assurance. Before the night and the flight were over, Linda—right there on the plane—invited the Savior, Jesus Christ, into her life. She has since become Wayne's prayer partner and is growing in her newfound faith, discovered in the middle of the night, like the jailer, because Wayne was ready to witness!

Are you ready at a moment's notice to share the gospel with people who exhibit open, receptive hearts? Perhaps you should consider taking the Evangelism Explosion training which prepared Wayne to be a ready witness.

Acts 16 is one of the best chapters in the Bible

to illustrate the evangelistic theme of . . .

5. *Oikos* outreach

It is both interesting and significant that God first saved Lydia and then, through Lydia's influence, the others in her *oikos*—her natural network of relationships. And so it was with the Philippian jailer. Notice first . . .

a. Lydia and her household

> When [Lydia] and the members of her household were baptized, she invited us to her home. "If you consider me a believer in the Lord," she said, "come and stay at my house." And she persuaded us. (16:15)

Evidently Lydia was a proselyte, that is, a Gentile from Asia who had moved to Philippi and become a worshiper of Israel's God the Lord. Her heart was open to the things of God and she responded to the invitation to trust Christ as Savior. Then the rest of her household also trusted Christ and were baptized. Something similar happened to . . .

b. The jailer and his household

> [Paul and Silas] replied, "Believe in the Lord Jesus, and you will be saved— you and your household." Then they spoke the word of the Lord to him and

to all the others in his house. At that hour of the night the jailer took them and washed their wounds; then immediately he and all his family were baptized. The jailer brought them into his house and set a meal before them; he was filled with joy because he had come to believe in God—he and his whole family. (16:31-34)

God used the earthquake to open the jailer's heart, and Paul and Silas led him to faith in Christ. His entire household also trusted Christ and were baptized.

You will remember from what I said earlier in this book that *household* in the Greek language means more than the immediate family. It usually included friends, relatives, associates and neighbors. Thus, we see again the gospel spreading along the responsive lines of personal relationships.

One day a member of our congregation dropped by my office.

"Thank you, Pastor Tom," he said, "for training me in EE! This past week my wife's uncle, who was like a stepdad to her, passed away. But before he died my wife, Becky, asked me to visit him and share the gospel with him.

"My evangelistic skills were just a bit rusty so I got out my EE textbook and reviewed the presentation. When I thought I was as prepared as I could be, I went to the hospital to visit our critically ill uncle. He was ready. As I shared the good news of Jesus with him, he responded in faith. Today he is in the presence of the Lord!"

I was so glad that John was equipped for such a vital ministry. But I also realized that no one can reach a person's relatives better than someone in that person's network of trust relationships.

Have you drawn up a list of your friends, relatives, associates and neighbors? Do you pray daily for them by name? Are you building bridges to them? What are you doing to redemptively reach out to them?

Have you shared the gospel with any of them yet? Has any of them professed faith in Christ yet? What are you doing to nurture them in their newfound faith?

Discussion Questions

1. Why do you think it's true that knowing there are many, many people searching for God will greatly motivate Christians to witness?

2. From your experience, what are some of the circumstances that God brings into people's lives to open their hearts to the gospel?

3. What are some of the circumstances that Satan employs to close people's hearts to the

gospel? What can we do about such circumstances? What place do you think prayer might have in such situations?

4. What do you understand a vision to mean? Is it possible today for a Christian to have a vision?

5. If someone like the Philippian jailer were to say to you, "What must I do to be saved?" could you give him or her a clear presentation of the gospel? What would you say?

6. Could you bring such a person to a definite decision of trusting Christ as his or her Savior? How would you do it?

7. What is your understanding of God's part and the evangelist's part in bringing a person to Christ?

Chapter Seven

Witnessing in Your World

John 1:1-47

WHEN JESUS COMMANDED His followers to "go and make disciples of all nations" (Matthew 28:19), He certainly didn't mean for every individual to evangelize every other individual in every nation of the world! That, of course, would be impossible!

Rather, I believe Jesus saw the world as a gigantic mosaic comprising millions of little networks of people. He expected each believer to witness to his or her contacts with the intent of winning to Him as many of them as possible.

If every believer did, in fact, witness to those in his or her "world," and if he or she faithfully discipled those new Christians until they repeated the witness in *their* networks of relationships, the world would be evangelized quite speedily and effectively.

Elise, a lovely wife, mother and homemaker, enlisted in our EE training and was assigned to my team. Her last name began with the letter "E," so I jokingly assured her that with her initials I would do my best to equip her to become a star witness in our EE ministry. She studied hard, learned her material well, came to every class thoroughly prepared. But she had one problem: as a homemaker she felt she didn't have any opportunities to "witness as a way of life." Shut up at home with only her children, she couldn't see any possible occasion for meeting non-Christians with whom she might share the gospel.

So I suggested that she ask God to bring some people to her. God answered in an amazing way! One day a Kirby vacuum cleaner saleswoman came through her neighborhood and knocked on her door.

"I have a gift for you," the woman said, "if you'll let me come in for a few minutes." And then she added, "But first I have a short presentation for you."

"Come on in," Elise responded enthusiastically. "I have a gift and a presentation for you, too!" When the Kirby saleswoman had finished her presentation and attempted to close the sale, Elise said, "I never make a purchase of this size without consulting my husband, Gary.

Let me call him at work. It will just take a minute." Gary said he'd have to think about it—and pray. He'd call back in a few minutes. So while they waited, Elise asked permission to share her presentation about the gift of eternal life.

Just as she came to the commitment part, Gary called back. He told Elise he didn't feel they could afford the vacuum cleaner at that time. Elise dutifully passed this decision on to the Kirby saleswoman, sure that she would lose interest in the gospel. But she didn't! She listened right to the end and prayed to invite Christ into her life right there in Elise's living room.

Elise came to the next class all aglow. She told us of her divine appointment. She had discovered her "world" where God had placed her for a witness. Well equipped through EE, she was able to pass on the most wonderful gift of all—abundant, eternal life through Jesus Christ.

To win your "world," you must witness to Christ by both your life and your lips. John 1:1-47 underscores the thesis.

Although John 1 might be outlined in a number of different ways, from the perspective of friendship evangelism I shall divide it into three parts: (1) the WORD (your message), (2) the WITNESS (you, the messenger) and (3) the WORLD (your network of relationships). First let's see what John says about . . .

1. The Word

As witnesses you and I must have a message, and John tells us that our message is "the Word"—Jesus Christ. John sets forth two very basic facets of Jesus the Message: His identity and His ministry.

a. His identity

Jesus was both God and Man. He was the infinite God. He was also Man—human. Here is what John says about His deity:

> In the beginning was the Word, and the Word was with God, and the Word was God. He was with God in the beginning.
>
> Through him all things were made; without him nothing was made that has been made. In him was life, and that life was the light of men. The light shines in the darkness, but the darkness has not understood it. (John 1:1-5)

Clearly Jesus, the Word, is God—Co-creator and Sustainer of all things, including life itself!

Then John writes about Christ's humanity:

> The Word became flesh and made his dwelling among us. We have seen his glory, the glory of the One and Only,

who came from the Father, full of
grace and truth. (1:14)

John tells us that God became Man in Jesus
Christ. He lived on this earth among human
beings who saw His glory.

b. His ministry

Even as Jesus' being was twofold, God and
Man, so what He did was twofold. He revealed
and He redeemed.

Jesus revealed God to man. "No one has ever
seen God, but God the One and Only, who is at
the Father's side, has made him known" (1:18).

Jesus is called the Word. The metaphor is rich
in meaning. You and I use words to reveal the
invisible thoughts in our minds and the invisible affections of our hearts. In the same
way, our invisible God sent His Son Jesus to
express to us His thoughts, affections, nature
and will. People are constantly claiming that
they would believe in God if they could see
God! Jesus the Word became flesh so that John
and others could declare, "We have seen his
glory, the glory of the One and Only." Jesus
came to reveal God to us!

He also came to redeem us. "The next day
John saw Jesus coming toward him and said,
'Look, the Lamb of God, who takes away the
sin of the world!' " (1:29).

Every Jewish boy and girl grew up understanding the meaning of a lamb in God's

scheme of things. A lamb was used for sacrifices. It was offered in the place of the one sacrificing it. The lamb's blood paid the penalty for sin. It brought forgiveness and salvation. So when John introduced Jesus as God's Lamb Who had come to take away the sin of the world, the message was clear. In John's eyes, Jesus was the promised Redeemer.

So that is Who Jesus was then and Who He is today! Jesus is the infinite God-man Who came to reveal God to us and redeem us from our sins. What a wonderful Word! What a wonderful message you and I have to share.

2. The witness

> There came a man who was sent from God; his name was John. He came as a witness to testify concerning that light, so that through him all men might believe. (1:6-7)

A message needs a messenger. A word must have a voice to proclaim that word. God sent John the Baptist as a witness. As God sent John to witness, so He sends you and me to witness. In fact, let me suggest, if you are in the habit of marking your Bible, that you cross out the name *John* and put in the margin next to verse 6 *your* first name so that it will read, "There came a man [or woman] sent from God whose name was [your name]."

If you've ever studied this chapter carefully,

you've probably noticed that John has a unique writing style. He is not orderly and logical like Paul. In fact, it is sometimes difficult to follow his thoughts. Here he alternates his subject, first speaking of Jesus, then of John the Baptist. But that is not an accident! There is reason for such an arrangement in the text. God sent *both* Jesus and John the Baptist, the Word and the witness, and their ministries were interdependent.

This can best be illustrated by referring to the two chief metaphors of the chapter: *Word* in 1:14 and *voice*, which John calls himself in 1:23. We illustrate the interdependence of Word and voice when we read the Scriptures or sing a chorus. If it is to be heard, a word needs a voice. If it is to be meaningful, a voice must convey a word. As a word needs a voice, so John needed Jesus for salvation and Jesus needed John to witness to that salvation. "[John the Baptist] came as a witness to testify concerning that light, so that through him all men might believe" (1:7).

Notice in the above verse that the witness aims to bring people to belief! And so a true witness is always concerned about his credibility. Thus his Christian life is very important.

The Chinese have a very interesting character for the word *believe*. It looks something like this:

As you know, their characters are picture symbols of the words they convey. This particular character for believe is composed of two picture symbols. The one on the right is the character for *word* and the one on the left is the character for *man*. In their symbolism they are saying that belief is dependent upon a man's life aligning with his lips; his walk must match his words.

Suzanne came to the information center of our church one Sunday morning to tell Miles what an impact his friendship evangelism had had both on her life and on people where she works.

It began with the passing of our "Friendship Book," a red book that is passed down the pew from aisle to aisle at the time of the offering. People are to sign the book and pass it on. Visitors are requested to include their address as well. When everyone in the row has signed, the book is returned to its starting place. Each person in the pew is encouraged to look at the signatures, matching names with faces.

Miles makes a habit of checking the book to see if there are any visitors in his row. At the end of the service he goes out of his way to greet them and invite them to our visitor reception. Then, having copied the names and addresses from the friendship book, he goes home and writes personal notes to the visitors, thanking them for their visit and inviting them to come back.

Suzanne related to Miles how much that personal touch had meant to her. After Miles' warm contact, she kept coming back every service until one Sunday, after Pastor Bob's message, she prayed to receive Christ as her Savior.

Suzanne went on to tell Miles that recently at First Tier Bank where she works and where for a few years Miles served as vice president, she heard a most dynamic testimony. A fellow employee named Kent shared with those who were gathered that he had watched the life and walk of one of the vice presidents named Miles. He asked Miles one day what made him so different. Miles invited him to meet him for breakfast and shared Jesus Christ with him. Right there at the breakfast table Kent invited Christ into his life and began to experience the same life changing grace of God.

What was Miles's secret? He focused his attention on *being* before *doing* and *witnessing*. He made sure that his life and lips gave forth the same message. And his life attracted Kent to Christ.

So what kind of life must you have if you are to witness effectively? What are the characteristics of a life that will attract people to Christ?

Returning to John 1, I note that the writer goes on to describe the life of the believable witness. He enumerates four traits essential to an effective witness. To be Christ's witness you need to meet these four conditions:

a. Be born of God

> Yet to all who received him, to those
> who believed in his name, he gave the
> right to become children of God—
> children born not of natural descent,
> nor of human decision or a husband's
> will, but born of God. (1:12-13)

You must be born again. When Christ came
into the world, not everyone trusted Him for
salvation; but those who did were born into
God's family.

There is a heresy that has crept into many
churches today called universalism. This
heresy often uses such nice sounding phrases
as "the fatherhood of God and the brotherhood
of man." It teaches that by virtue of creation we
are all children in God's happy family. But
God's Word has quite a different message. It
declares people are only His children by personal faith in Christ.

Later Jesus talks to Nicodemus (John 3), a
man who was religious, rich and a ruler. Jesus
told him he had to be born again, or he would
never see the kingdom of God. To be a witness
you, too, must first be born again.

I was in Edmonton, Alberta, for an evangelistic weekend with Vietnamese settlers. I was
staying with Pastor Thanh and his family. The
pastor's three sons gathered with their dad and
me at the dining room table for breakfast. The

oldest of the three boys was Christopher. Having been born in Canada, Christopher spoke fluent English, so I said to him—in English—"Christopher, you have a beautiful name!"

Christopher looked a little surprised, so I continued. "Did you know that you have *Christ* in your name?" I don't think he had thought about it that way, so I pursued the point further.

"Christopher, let me ask you, with a name like yours, do you have Christ in your *heart*?"

Suddenly, he realized what I had been leading up to and seemed pleased to have an opportunity to tell me that, yes, he'd been to his uncle's funeral in Portland and on the way home in the car he was thinking a lot about death. He asked his pastor-father how his uncle knew for sure he was going to heaven. His father shared the simple plan of salvation. When they pulled off the interstate at a rest stop, he asked his dad to help him pray to receive Christ.

"Right there," Christopher said jubilantly, "I received Christ into my heart by faith!" It was a beautiful, clear testimony of how he had been "born of God."

Later that morning in my message to the Vietnamese congregation, I could see there were a lot of children and youth in the service, so I related my breakfast table conversation with Christopher. I told them that Christopher was a child of God going to heaven, not because he was the pastor's son, but because he had Christ in his heart. I asked them if they had Christ in their hearts. I invited any who wanted to be born into God's family to come forward. I've seldom seen such a beautiful sight as one after another of those youth and children came forward, lining the front altar railing of the church. I invited their parents to come and stand beside them. I soon would be leaving Edmonton, but their moms and dads could help them in their newfound faith.

Do *you* have Christ in your heart? Have you been born a second time—this time born of God, born into God's family? If not, read again verses 12 and 13 and by simple faith in Christ invite Him into your life as your Savior and Lord!

That's the first step in becoming an effective witness for Christ. The next step is to . . .

b. Behold

> The Word became flesh and made his dwelling among us. We have seen his glory, the glory of the One and Only, who came from the Father, full of grace and truth. . . .
>
> John [the Baptist] gave this testimony: "I saw the Spirit come down from heaven as a dove and remain on him. I would not have known him, ex-

cept that the one who sent me to baptize with water told me, 'The man on
whom you see the Spirit come down
and remain is he who will baptize
with the Holy Spirit.' I have seen and I
testify that this is the Son of God."
(1:14, 32-34)

The dictionary defines a witness as one who
has personal knowledge of a thing. In our
courts of law a witness must be able to say, "I
saw," or "I was there." John the Apostle and
John the Baptist say over and over that they
saw. They were credible witnesses.

Of course, first century witnesses such as
John the Baptist and John the Apostle, living in
Palestine, had opportunity to see Jesus. But
what about you and me who are living 2,000
years later? How can we behold Jesus Christ?

In Second Corinthians Paul tells us that we
can contemplate the glory of the Lord: "And
we, who with unveiled faces all reflect [mar-
ginal reading: *contemplate*] the Lord's glory, are
being transformed into his likeness with ever-
increasing glory, which comes from the Lord,
who is the Spirit" (3:18). As you and I study the
life of Christ in the Word day after day, His
glory begins to reflect from our lives. And we
become ever more credible witnesses.

Again, this is why relational evangelism is
more effective than one-time-encounter evangelism. People with whom we have an ex-

tended relationship have opportunity to see Christ in our lives and are much more apt to believe in Him.

One day at work Lori saw something different in her work associate. Since I can't remember her name, I'll call her Jeannie. Lori saw in Jeannie a new joy, an unusual buoyancy of spirit, apparent purity and honesty. Lori thought to herself, "Did Jeannie get a new boyfriend? Maybe a raise? A better apartment?"

When Lori asked Jeannie why she was so different, Jeannie replied that she had trusted Christ as her Savior and had been born again.

"How can I do that?" Lori wanted to know. But because it was all so new to Jeannie and because she had no church background, she didn't know what to say. She got her Bible and fumbled through page after page. But alas, she couldn't find the verses someone had shared with her. She apologized for not being able to help Lori.

That night, however, there was a knock on Lori's door and Jim from our church, with questionnaire in hand, led Lori to faith in Christ.

The point I want to illustrate is that something dynamic had happened to Jeannie when she trusted Christ. Not only had she been born again, but she evidently had glimpsed Christ. Her life had been changed, and her new demeanor was what got Lori's attention and prepared the way for Jim's witness.

c. Be full

> From the fullness of his grace we have
> all received one blessing after another.
> For the law was given through Moses;
> grace and truth came through Jesus
> Christ. (1:16-17)

To be Christ's witness you must also be full of His grace. *Grace* is a rich word. Grace means God's unmerited favor. As someone put it, it is *God's riches at Christ's expense.* It is God's free forgiveness of your sins and His gift of eternal life that you receive at the point of salvation. But it is also much more!

Grace is the moral and social beauty we receive from God's indwelling Spirit. It is the divine power and authority granted by the Holy Spirit to be an effective witness. It is what Christ promised when He said to His disciples, "You will receive power when the Holy Spirit comes on you, and you will be my witnesses . . . to the ends of the earth" (Acts 1:8).

I cannot help but believe the sequence in John 1:17 is significant: first grace, then truth. It is possible for you to be full of truth—gospel outlines, Bible verses, illustrations, logic, sound theology, impeccable apologetics. But having all that great storehouse of truth, your witness will be ineffective if you lack God's grace in your life. The wealth of truth in your head must be accompanied by an abundance of grace in your heart.

In his Gospel, Matthew describes John the Baptist and his teaching ministry (see Matthew 3). It is quite evident that John didn't study in one of our evangelical seminaries or Bible colleges. According to our procedures, he did everything wrong!

Today students are taught to go where the people are. John went into the sparsely inhabited desert (3:1). Seminarians today are counseled to read *Dress for Success*—to identify with the business and professional people to whom they hope to minister. John was content to wear camel's hair garments (3:4). We feed our visiting evangelists well. John subsisted on locusts and wild honey (3:4). Student preachers today are told to begin their sermon with complimentary words to put the audience in a good frame of mind. John opened his message by calling his audience a "brood of vipers!" (3:7). If you look closely at his whole message, you will find nothing in it calculated to win friends and influence people. He preached repentance, wrath to come and unquenchable judgment fire (3:7-12).

But people turned out in unbelievable numbers to see and hear John the Baptist. They confessed their sins. They begged him to baptize them.

What was John's secret? Was it not that he was full of God's grace? God's grace, resting upon John the Baptist, attracted people to God.

There's just no substitute for being *full*—full of grace. It has been said that Christianity is "better caught than taught." This happens when people see the grace of God and the beauty of Christ in your life and then listen to the truth of your message. Grace must accompany—better yet, it must prepare the way for—truth.

d. Be vocal

> The next day John [the Baptist] saw Jesus coming toward him and said, "Look, the Lamb of God, who takes away the sin of the world! (1:29)
>
> . . . When he saw Jesus passing by, he said, "Look, the Lamb of God!" (1:36)

There are Christians who absolve themselves from sharing the gospel by rationalizing, "I witness by my life; what really counts is my walk." Such a philosophy sounds commendable, but it's just not biblical. John the Baptist over and over verbalized his witness.

Jesus commanded His followers to "preach [announce] the good news to all creation" (Mark 16:15). Luke tells us that Jerusalem believers, because of severe persecution, were "scattered" everywhere and that they "preached [announced] the word wherever they went" (Acts 8:1, 4). Paul asks, "How can they believe in the one of whom they have not heard? And how can they hear without someone preaching to them?" (Romans 10:14).

Someone has aptly observed that when people witness only with their lives, they witness only to themselves; but when they witness with their lips, they witness to Jesus Christ. Without question, Jesus expects His followers to witness verbally.

But what will you say when the opportunity comes to be vocal? Some Christians are tongue-tied, paralyzed with fear. Others haven't been trained properly to lead someone to Christ.

Jack has a toy business. His salesmen cover a wide territory around Omaha. One of his salesmen, Randy, worked for Jack about a year. They got to be good friends and enjoyed a close working relationship. One day on the way back to the office after lunch, Randy shared with Jack about his pagan background. He had almost never been to church. So Jack asked him if he would like to know more about Christ. Before the conversation ended, Randy had prayed to receive Christ and is today in church every Sunday.

Jack is always ready when the Lord opens the door. He has been trained in our evangelism equipping ministry. And many of his friends, knowing how graciously vocal Jack is with the gospel, call him when they need help. A few weeks ago one of Jack's friends was working out with a bodybuilding friend named Jason. Jason was a construction worker who had grown up in the Catholic church. But he didn't know how to get to heaven. So he asked Jack's friend to help him. Unable to explain her faith, Jack's friend called Jack to see if he could come over and meet with Jason in her apartment. At the end of the evening, bodybuilding Jason knew he was going to heaven!

If you are not able to verbalize your witness, sign up for evangelism training at your church and purchase some *Do You Know for Sure?* tracts from Evangelism Explosion International. If necessary, get a witnessing friend to help you. But don't leave your unsaved friends without a vocal witness!

To summarize, to be an effective witness you need to be born again, you need to behold, you need to be full of grace and you need to be vocal.

3. The world

> The true light that gives light to every man was coming into the world.
>
> He was in the world, and though the world was made through him, the world did not recognize him. (1:9-10)

> "Look, the Lamb of God, who takes away the sin of the world!" (1:29)

Jesus came into the world, but the world did not know Him. He came to take away the sin of the world. Hence His followers were called, trained and sent to be His witnesses in the world.

Too often that word *world* conjures pictures of overseas missions: the Bobo of Africa, the Dani of Irian Jaya or the Raday of Vietnam. While it is true that we are to send missionaries to reach every tongue, tribe and nation with the gospel, the world for each of us is much closer. Notice that the world for Jesus and His followers began with those persons within the circle of their personal relationships.

a. **Relatives: Jesus won His cousin.**

> [Jesus] came to that which was his own, but his own did not receive him. Yet to all who received him, to those who believed in his name, he gave the right to become children of God— children born not of natural descent, nor of human decision or a husband's will, but born of God. (1:11-13)

> The next day, John [the Baptist] saw Jesus coming toward him and said, "Look, the Lamb of God, who takes away the sin of the world!" (1:29)

Jesus' mother, Mary, and John's mother, Elizabeth, were blood related, although we don't know precisely the relationship. When Jesus "came to that which was his own, . . . his own did not receive him." But some did, for the next verse says, "To all who received him, to those who believed in his name, he gave the right to become children of God." John the Baptist was certainly one of those who believed, for he testifies to his faith in Jesus (see 1:29, 34). Evidently Jesus had witnessed to His earthly cousin and brought him to saving faith.

Pattie and Suzie visited their aunt over Thanksgiving weekend. As they were taking their first bite of turkey, their aunt asked, "Well, what are you girls up to there in Omaha?" One of the two replied, "We're doing EE, Auntie." And, of course, their aunt wanted to know what EE was.

"Oh, we begin by asking folks a couple of very interesting questions, Auntie," the other girl responded.

"And why don't you ask me the questions?" their aunt suggested. She gave a works oriented answer, so before too far into the meal the sisters were sharing the gospel with her. To their great delight their aunt received Christ before the day had passed. And the girls had one of the most thankful Thanksgivings of their lives.

God has given you a trust relationship with your relatives. They are part of your "world" that Christ wants you to reach for Him.

b. Associates: John led his followers to Christ.

The next day John was there again

> with two of his disciples. When he
> saw Jesus passing by, he said, "Look,
> the Lamb of God!"
> When the two disciples heard him
> say this, they followed Jesus. (1:35-37)

Even as John was associated with his disciples in his daily work, so you and I have associates—fellow employees, staff members, team members—with whom we mix on a daily basis. As we cultivate a trustful relationship with them, we also may be used of God to bring them to Christ. We may want to deepen the relationship by inviting them to our home for a barbecue, by taking a fishing trip together, by planning a day of shopping together. Then, as God prepares the way we can share the gospel with them or invite them to church to hear the gospel.

Wayne is a widower who supports himself as a welder. But he views his work place as part of the "world" to whom Christ has sent him. He has seen quite a number of his fellow welders put their trust in Christ. One of them, Kevin, was a Roman Catholic, so when Wayne shared Christ with him over the lunch hour, he said he'd have to check what Wayne told him with the priest. Furthermore, the priest could take care of his sins at the confessional!

However, Kevin wasn't satisfied with the priest's explanation. Several months later he sought out Wayne to talk further. He asked

Wayne to pray for him and his sins. Instead, Wayne suggested that Kevin could himself go direct to Jesus. In fact, Jesus was willing to come into his life and change it, so he wouldn't have to live a life of constant sinning followed by constant confessing. That day Kevin trusted Christ and started attending a gospel preaching church in his town just south of Omaha.

Some weeks later Wayne was reading the Omaha newspaper and saw a photo of a wrecked pick-up truck. On the ground next to the truck was the body of the driver—Kevin! Wayne visited the funeral home to comfort Kevin's wife with the good news that Kevin was in heaven. She said that she had noticed a marked change in Kevin and wondered what had happened. Kevin's mother was getting ready to pay the church some money to pray Kevin into heaven and was overjoyed when Wayne told her that Kevin was already in heaven. Right there in the funeral home Kevin's mother prayed to trust Christ.

As we pray by name for our work associates, build loving relationships with them, invite them to various church activities and share our personal testimonies and the gospel with them, God will bring many of them under His saving grace.

c. Family: Andrew brought his brother to Christ.

Andrew, Simon Peter's brother, was

one of the two who heard what John
had said and who had followed Jesus.
The first thing Andrew did was to
find his brother Simon and tell him,
"We have found the Messiah" (that is,
the Christ). And he brought him to
Jesus. (1:40-42)

Here in John 1 is still another type of relationship that lends itself to gospel witness.
Andrew, after his life-changing encounter with
Jesus, remembered that he had a brother who
might be open to a similar experience. Andrew
brought his brother, Simon Peter, to Christ.

Over and over in New Testament times we
find Christians winning their family members
to Christ. When the Philippian jailer trusted
Christ as Savior, his entire "household" also
came to Christ.

**d. Neighbors: Philip probably was Andrew
and Peter's neighbor.**

The next day Jesus decided to leave
for Galilee. Finding Philip, he said to
him, "Follow me." (1:43)

Philip, Andrew and Peter all lived in Bethsaida. Bethsaida was not a large place. There is
every reason, therefore, to presume that Philip
was a neighbor to Andrew and Peter.

In introducing this chapter, I referred to Elise,
with the initials EE, who lamented that as a

homemaker she had few non-Christian contacts with whom she could share the gospel. Shortly after the Kirby vacuum cleaner salesperson came to her door, her unsaved brother-in-law, Jim, came to spend Christmas with Elise's family. Elise spent time enhancing her relationship with Jim, earning the right to share the gospel with him. She prayed that God would give her an opportunity to talk with him about Jesus. One day she found him alone and asked if she might share with him something wonderful God had done for her. Jim was very open and ended up giving his heart to Christ.

Not too long after that a new family moved into the house next door. Elise baked a cake and invited Karla, her new neighbor, to come over for a cup of coffee. They visited extensively and became well acquainted. When Elise shared with Karla her personal testimony and then the gospel, Karla trusted Christ as her personal Savior. Elise discovered that even for homemakers, there are fruitful opportunities to share her faith.

You can never know all that God has in mind through your witness. One day a Christian woman in California looked out her kitchen window and saw a moving van pull into the driveway of the house across the street. "New neighbors!" she thought to herself and got busy in her kitchen baking a cake. When the cake was cool and properly frosted, she took it across the street to welcome the new family to California and her neighborhood. She learned that the Prices had some very fine sons. Later that week her husband met Mr. Price at the bus stop where together they were leaving for work. Relationships developed between the neighbors and one happy day the Prices gave their hearts to the Lord and started attending church with their friendly neighbors.

As the years passed two of the Prices' sons, Wendell and Roy, entered the Christian ministry, becoming very successful pastors. Wendell eventually became president of Alliance Theological Seminary in Nyack, New York. Little could this faithful woman, eager to befriend new neighbors and share the gospel with them, have guessed the full outcome!

You, too, can build relationships with people on your block or in your neighborhood. As you pray for them and seek to reach them for Christ, God will use you to impact some of them for eternity.

e. Friends: Philip was Nathanael's friend and introduced him to his Savior.

> Philip found Nathanael and told him, "We have found the one Moses wrote about in the Law, and about whom the prophets also wrote—Jesus of Nazareth, the son of Joseph."
>
> "Nazareth! Can anything good come

from there?" Nathanael asked.

"Come and see," said Philip.

When Jesus saw Nathanael approaching, he said of him, "Here is a true Israelite, in whom there is nothing false." (1:45-47)

The best thing you can do for your friends is to share your Savior with them. In fact, a true friend will be concerned for the spiritual welfare of those he or she loves the most and will do everything possible to bring them to Christ.

Denise jogs in her neighborhood to keep in shape. She built a warm friendship with her neighbor Chris by jogging with her. One day as the two were jogging together Chris said to Denise, "There's something different about you and I can't figure out what it is." Denise's Christ-life was showing through, and Chris wanted whatever it was that made Denise such a beautiful person! Unfortunately, Denise hadn't been equipped like her husband, Tom, to share her faith. So she told Chris that when she had a little more time she would tell her the secret.

"I've gotta sign up for EE," Denise announced to Tom that night. "I need to share Christ with Chris."

About 13 weeks into the next semester of EE, Denise felt adequately prepared. As they were jogging one morning, Denise reminded Chris of her question and asked if they could sit down on the curb and talk. That morning Chris discovered what made Denise different. More important, she received the same Savior Who had changed Denise into the lovely Christian she is!

Do you realize that you may be the only true Christian your friends, relatives, associates and neighbors know? They are the world into which Jesus Christ sends you with His Word to witness. No one can witness to everyone in the world. But as you adopt your segment of that world and as others adopt their segments, the whole world will hear of Jesus. Just as He commanded!

Discussion Questions

1. What is the significance of John's calling Jesus the "Word"? What does John tell us about His nature?

2. John the Baptist calls himself a "voice" (1:23). Of what significance is that?

3. What biblical traits do you feel should mark the life of a person bent on winning people to Christ in our day?

4. What if Jesus should tell you that you are His personal representative in your neighborhood, place of employment, club, school, home? How would you respond? What would you do?

5. Of all your unsaved friends, relatives, work or school associates or neighbors, who would you say is the most open to the gospel? What are some of the things you might do to begin reaching out to him or her?

6. If the way should open for you to share the gospel with that person, what do you think you would do or say? Could you share the gospel effectively?

Chapter Eight

Reaching "Households" for Christ

Acts 10

O N A FLIGHT BACK TO the United States from visiting my son and daughter-in-law, Jeff and Beth, in China, I found myself sitting next to Cleveland. Cleveland told me he was from New York City. Later I heard him engaged in a non-English conversation with a fellow passenger. When I asked him what language he had been using, he told me it was Portuguese. Cleveland was married to a Brazilian, had spent many years in Brazil and had a brother-in-law who was an evangelical pastor there.

I hardly needed a better opening than that!

"Have *you* found a faith?" I asked.

"No," Cleveland admitted, "but I'm looking for one." I asked if I might pursue my questions, promising Cleveland I had some wonderful news to share with him. And during the flight from Hong Kong to Tokyo, I had the joy of helping Cleveland discover eternal life in Jesus Christ.

God has clearly promised through His prophet Jeremiah, "You will seek me and find me when you seek me with all your heart" (Jeremiah 29:13). Cleveland clearly fit the category of a "seeker." Perhaps his evangelical brother-in-law had sown the seed. No doubt other believers had watered that seed with their prayers. And I, on that flight from Hong Kong to Tokyo, experienced the thrill of harvesting the fruit, leading Cleveland to Christ.

To fulfill the promise He made through Jeremiah, God needs His people to actively help seeking people find Him! Alas, there are more non-Christians seeking after God than there are Christians helping them find Him. Many times a new believer, after receiving Christ, will exclaim, "This is wonderful! But why did it take me so long to find this out? Why didn't somebody tell me sooner?"

The sad fact of the matter is that many, many Christians, having experienced difficulty in sharing the wonderful message of the gospel, have thereafter supposed that "no one out there is interested." Having encountered a little opposition or rejection, they now surmise that non-Christians just aren't searching for the truth. They assume that people in general aren't really open to God or His marvelous saving grace.

I took an evangelism team to a shopping mall in Nanuet, New York, to do some "questionnaire" evangelism. On the way to the mall one of my team members was telling me how many people in his circle of friends were resistant to the gospel. It was as though he was preparing me for a similar response at the mall.

In a matter of five minutes, we met a young man, Steve, in a wheelchair. Steve appeared to be friendless and lonely. We first engaged him in small talk to build rapport. After we had gained his trust, we asked Steve if we might share the gospel with him. That day Steve prayed to receive Christ. Afterwards he thanked us and promised to follow through with his newfound faith.

As we were about to leave the mall to return home, another young man, Robert, stopped us in the entryway.

"Do you happen to have a light?" he wanted to know. We told him we had neither lighter nor matches.

"By the way, what are you doing in the mall?" he asked, his curiosity piqued by the papers we were carrying.

"We have been doing a questionnaire," we

said. Robert expressed interest, so we took time to go through the questionnaire with him. Before we were finished, Robert, too, had prayed to invite Christ into his life.

"You know," he said, "I had a feeling that God was going to talk to me through you when I first saw you here!"

Later that evening my team member who was apprehensive about anyone being interested in the gospel prayed, "God, I repent for thinking that no one is interested in Your gospel. Help me to be faithful in going out with Your good news, knowing that there are many people seeking You and Your salvation!"

Yes, people *are* seeking God. Both the Scriptures and experience testify that the prevailing contrary opinion is an extremely dangerous misconception. There are in fact many people all around you and me who are seeking after God, trying to find the Truth, longing for salvation and eternal life! And of all who are seeking, *those within your own "household" are possibly your most fruitful evangelistic contacts.*

So in this chapter I want to further pursue the theme of "household" evangelism. To do this, I need to deal with three important factors in your life: (1) your household, (2) your hang-ups and (3) your helpers. I turn to Acts 10 to examine these three factors as the apostle Peter reached out to God-seeking Cornelius.

1. Your household

> At Caesarea there was a man named
> Cornelius, a centurion in what was
> known as the Italian Regiment. He
> and all his family were devout and
> God-fearing; he gave generously to
> those in need and prayed to God
> regularly. (10:1-2)

Notice that Cornelius was a gentile military
leader who with his family was searching after
God. By that I mean he respected God, gave
generously to needy people around him and
prayed regularly to God. Only a person who
was truly seeking God would do those things
and thus be ripe for the message of the gospel.

Notice that "all his family" joined him in this
ardent search after God. In the New American
Standard Version, "family" is more accurately
translated "household." Again, it is the Greek
word *oikos*, which has a much broader meaning
than one's immediate family members. It includes friends, relatives, associates and neighbors. In fact, as you read on in Acts 10 you will
notice that Luke, the human author of Acts,
under the inspiration of the Holy Spirit refers
to all four of these people groups who com-
prised Cornelius's *oikos*. Look with me more
closely at each groups, which we have come to
refer to as "FRAN"—*f*riends, *r*elatives, *as*-
sociates and *n*eighbors. We begin with . . .

a. Your associates

> When the angel who spoke to him
> had gone, Cornelius called two of his
> servants and a devout soldier who
> was one of his attendants. (10:7)

Note that Cornelius's *oikos* or household included soldiers and servants. These were
people with whom he associated in his daily
work routine. Our present-day equivalent
might be employees or employer, regular customers, barber or hairdresser, insurance agent,
auto mechanic, bank teller, diet counselor, shoe
repairman, mailman. They are people with
whom you relate on a somewhat regular basis,
whom you know well or ought to get to know
better.

Dean and Don were riding together, as they
often did, to call on some of their company's
regular customers. Dean had noticed that
Don's life-style was different from the other
salespeople. He exhibited some very unusual
and attractive qualities. Somehow that day
their conversation turned to God and church
and spiritual values. This wasn't the first time
they had talked this way, but this particular
day Dean's intense search for truth and reality
would come to a conclusion. Before the two
salesmen reached their first call, Dean had
turned his life over to God and received His
gift of eternal life in Jesus Christ. Today Dean

and Don are both actively worshiping and serving God at Christ Community Church!

b. Your relatives

> The next day Peter started out with them. . . . The following day he arrived in Caesarea. Cornelius was expecting them and had called together his relatives . . . (10:23-24)

When Peter arrived at Cornelius' home, this gentile military officer already had his relatives assembled and waiting. These, of course, were not limited to his wife and children. The term *relatives*, then as now, included grandparents, grandchildren, aunts, uncles, cousins, in-laws and maybe even a few "shirttail" cousins.

You have a biblical responsibility to reach this segment of your world for Christ. They are your mission field! There's probably no one who can more effectively evangelize your relatives than you—not even the evangelism team or the pastor. That's because you have a personal relationship with them. From time to time you've had close contact with them. Through the years, you've earned credibility with them.

Mary loved her grandmother very much. From childhood she had spent many days and hours with her. She had shared the gospel with her grandmother but with no apparent response. Then one day Mary's grandmother went to the hospital for the last time. Mary knew that she didn't have long in this world and prayed for some time alone with her. In a few minutes God answered her prayer and she was able to share the plan of salvation one more time. This time Mary could tell by the joy that lit up her grandmother's face and the peace in her own heart that this loved one was passing into the presence of the Lord.

c. Your friends

> Cornelius . . . had called together his relatives and close friends. (10:24)

Along with his relatives Cornelius also summoned his "close friends." They no doubt were the people with whom Cornelius spent much of his free time, people with whom he shared common interests, sports or hobbies. Maybe they were his former schoolmates or fellow club members.

With whom do you spend your free time? With whom do you enjoy jogging, golfing, playing tennis or Scrabble? Can you list some of your schoolmates with whom you still keep in regular touch? Are you a member of a club? Do you go shopping with a few special persons?

Together with two Christian golf partners, Fred was at the first tee ready to hit his first ball when a friend came up and asked if he might make it a foursome. By the time the four reached the fifth hole, this friend noticed that the other three didn't swear or get mad when they made a bad shot. He asked if he could play with them again sometime.

"How would you like to spend forever with us?" Fred asked.

"You sound like my grandmother," the friend commented.

This led Fred to share his testimony and the gospel right there at the fifth tee. Before the four of them continued the game, Fred's friend knelt by the golf bench and gave his heart to Christ!

God has brought friends into your life for a purpose. As you enjoy valuable, sometimes unforgettable experiences together, don't forget that they too are part of the "world" in which God has placed you. They are another segment of your special mission field.

d. Your neighbors

> Talking with him, Peter went inside
> and found a large gathering of people.
> (10:27)

As Peter and Cornelius, conversing together, entered the latter's house, Peter discovered the large assembly that Cornelius had brought together. The Scriptures do not mention neighbors specifically, but it is hard to imagine that among Cornelius's friends, relatives and associations there were *not* some of his neighbors.

They had watched his life. They had seen his zeal toward God and his expressions of love to needy people. Whatever he was pursuing, they wanted it too!

Patti had built many bridges to her neighbor and developed a real trust relationship with her. Meanwhile Patti had enrolled in our Evangelism Explosion training and was in the last few weeks of her first 16-week semester.

Her assignment every week called for reciting her EE outline to someone else. Still single, she didn't have a spouse or a roommate. So she called upon her neighbor friend to help.

In the introduction part of the outline at the appropriate place, Patti asked her neighbor the two diagnostic questions and discovered that her neighbor had no hope of eternal life and was depending upon good works to gain God's favor.

As Patti presented the gospel, she noticed that her neighbor was unusually attentive. And when she came to the commitment section, her neighbor asked, "How did you know that this is exactly what I have been looking for?" To the delight of them both, Patti led her neighbor to faith in Christ.

You may never really know how much your neighbors are watching you. You can't fully comprehend what impact you are having on them. What are you doing to manifest Christ's love to them? Do you pray regularly for them? Have you ever invited them to do something fun with you—a barbecue? a fishing trip? a ball game or concert? a county fair or rodeo? Are you availing yourself of "seeker Sundays" to invite them to your church?

Our church has made available to our congregation a wonderful new opportunity to reach out to their friends, relatives, associates and neighbors. It's a direct mailing of culturally relevant reading material with updated information about our church and upcoming special events. It's another way to show them love and sow seeds of the gospel in their hearts and minds.

Remember, 75 to 90 percent of the people who come to Christ in America do so through the direct influence of their friends, relatives, associates and neighbors—that is, through the witness of someone or ones in their "household." So the first factor you'll need to deal with if you're going to effectively reach out to those around you who are seeking after God is your household. And the second factor is . . .

2. Your hang-ups

Peter and all his fellow Jews had hang-ups when it came to Gentiles. They didn't fraternize with Gentiles in any way, shape or size. Gentiles were unclean. In order to motivate Peter to take the gospel to God-seeking Cornelius, the Lord showed to Peter a very unusual vision:

> About noon . . . Peter went up on the

roof to pray. He became hungry and wanted something to eat, and while the meal was being prepared, he fell into a trance. He saw heaven opened and something like a large sheet being let down to earth by its four corners. It contained all kinds of four-footed animals, as well as reptiles of the earth and birds of the air. Then a voice told him, "Get up, Peter. Kill and eat."

"Surely not, Lord!" Peter replied. "I have never eaten anything impure or unclean."

The voice spoke to him a second time, "Do not call anything impure that God has made clean."

This happened three times, and immediately the sheet was taken back to heaven.

While Peter was wondering about the meaning of the vision, the men sent by Cornelius found out where Simon's house was and stopped at the gate. (10:9-17)

God fully intended to overcome Peter's prejudices and objections. God refused to take "No!" for an answer. He told Peter the emissaries from Cornelius had arrived; He commanded Peter to abandon his hang-ups and take the gospel to Cornelius, the seeking soldier.

When it comes to reaching lost people, most people tend to back away from their responsibility because of one or more hang-ups. They vindicate their apathy or inactivity with various excuses. They salve their consciences with any number of nice-sounding pretexts.

Are you, like Peter, hesitant to reach out to non-Christians? Is it because of . . .

a. . . . a fear of the unknown?

"Do not hesitate to go with them, for I have sent them" (10:20).

The Holy Spirit seemed to sense that on that Joppa rooftop Peter feared meeting the visitors who were awaiting him below.

Apprehension about the unknown comes naturally. Suppose the one I witness to is not interested. Will he or she reject me? If the person asks a difficult question, how will I answer? Maybe he has turned off God! What if she doesn't believe the Bible?

Notice that when Peter overcame his mental reservations and obeyed the Spirit, God led him to a house full of eager, seeking, friendly, responsive people. And if you, too, will step out in faith, you will be surprised to discover that among your friends, relatives, associates and neighbors there are people whom God's Spirit has prepared to receive the gospel.

b. . . . a time problem?

> Then Peter invited the men into the house to be his guests.
>
> The next day Peter started out with them, and some of the brothers from Joppa went along. The following day he arrived in Caesarea. Cornelius was expecting them and had called together his relatives and close friends. (10:23-24)

Notice that Peter's evangelistic trip to Caesarea consumed much time. In fact, Cornelius said (verse 30) it had been four days from the time the angel appeared to him until Peter's arrival. And it would be a few more days (verse 48) before Peter would return to Joppa.

Building in-depth relationships with non-Christians and earning the right to share Christ with them will take precious time. Someone has suggested that the kind of love essential to winning lost loved ones and friends is spelled T-I-M-E. Confronted with Christ's evangelistic mandate, do you sidestep it with a "Right now I'm just too busy"? Do you back away with a "One of these days I'm going to try that." Or do you excuse your complacency with a "Wow, I'm so over-involved already!"

Admit it. You find time to do what you really want to do. When I was a student at Nyack

College, I was extremely busy. I worked three nights a week until 2:00 in the morning. I carried a heavy academic schedule. I played guard on the varsity basketball team, sang in the college choir and in the college's Ambassador Quartet.

But one day I watched this beautiful blonde sophomore walk gracefully across the campus. I said to myself, "No matter how busy I am I've got to find time to meet that girl and get to know her." And, sure enough, the day soon came when I asked her if we could spend an evening together. At least once a week, sometimes twice a week, I found time to spend with her.

Today I'm an extremely busy outreach pastor. A 70-hour workweek is not uncommon for me. But every fall I still find time to attend Nebraska University football games. I build that time into my Saturday afternoon schedule. We call it priority. We all have priorities.

And if you are truly concerned for the eternal welfare of your friends, relatives, associates and neighbors, you will make their evangelization a priority in your schedule.

c. . . . a sense of inadequacy?

> As Peter entered the house, Cornelius met him and fell at his feet in reverence. But Peter made him get up. "Stand up," he said, "I am only a man myself." (10:25-26)

If anyone had reason to feel inadequate, it was uneducated, crass, impulsive Peter. After all, hadn't he denied Christ three times in the high priest's courtyard? But now filled with the Holy Spirit, Peter was fearlessly presenting the claims of Christ before a whole assembly of Cornelius' family and friends.

You too—if you will step out in faith in God's Spirit—can see your inadequacies swallowed up in His power. He will do for you what He did for Peter. Trust Him and prove His promises true!

d. . . . discomfort with non-Christians?

> [Peter] said to them: "You are well aware that it is against our law for a Jew to associate with a Gentile or visit him. But God has shown me that I should not call any man impure or unclean." (10:28)

Peter was tempted to wriggle out of his commission to introduce Christ to non-Christian Gentiles. He just had never associated with them before and no doubt was extremely uncomfortable entering their "territory." Worse yet, for him it was unlawful—or, at least, until then it had been unlawful.

If not alert, you too can get caught up in your "holy huddles," spending all of your time with Christians until you find it very awkward to relate properly with your non-Christian neighbors and work associates. What you need to do is become actively involved with non-Christians. Join a club. Volunteer for some type of regular civic involvement. Participate in a local PTA. In so doing aggressively seek to build meaningful friendships with people outside your church fellowship.

Now if you have clearly focused your attention on reaching your "household" and have dealt seriously with your individual hang-ups, you need to turn for added assistance to . . .

3. Your helpers

Did you know that God has surrounded you with valuable assistants? Don't try to "go it alone!" First, look for . . .

a. A hospitable fellow-believer

> Then Peter invited the men into the house to be his guests. (10:23)

It wasn't Peter's house. He too was a guest of Simon the tanner (verse 6). So it was a cooperative effort matching Peter's evangelistic gifts with Simon's gift of hospitality.

In friendship evangelism, the way you and other churchgoers treat visitors is very important. Their sense of welcome has a very great impact upon them and prepares them for your witness. In 1980, when I first arrived at Christ Community Church, the church did not have a very effective ministry to visitors. One day as I was calling on a visitor, I asked the person for his impressions of our church. He said no one greeted him. In fact, he felt very unwelcome. He did not intend to return.

I went back to the church and began to develop a very comprehensive, intensive visitor-relations ministry.

First, we have a large parking area reserved for visitors. Parking attendants as well as signs direct visitors to those reserved spots closest to our entrances. A greeter meets them in the parking lot as they get out of their cars and directs them to the main entrance. Friendly, well-trained greeters are stationed at each church entrance. A welcome center just inside offers them directions and assistance. Ushers greet them and escort them into the sanctuary or to the appropriate Sunday school class.

At a given point in the worship service a special welcome is extended to them. They are publicly invited to return. This invitation is reinforced in a letter from the senior pastor sent to them early in the week. We also send a friendly volunteer to their home with a loaf of banana or nut bread. The volunteer thanks them for their visit and invites them to return.

Upon their second visit they can expect a phone call from a volunteer couple who invite them to their home for a dessert evening. The volunteer couple and another church couple build bridges of friendship, explaining to them the various church activities, inviting them to return again.

Once a month, following the morning worship hour, we schedule a pot-luck dinner for all newcomers. We are prepared to answer any questions they may have. We want our visitors to know that we love them and wish to minister to them.

After their fourth appearance, visitors will get a call from the president of one of our adult Sunday school classes inviting them to Sunday school. In a large church it is important to incorporate them into a Sunday school class or other smaller group where they will build friendships, find their needs for fellowship met and also become recipients of the caring ministry which only a small group can extend.

Hospitality is important in reaching non-Christian friends. So look around to see if you can team up with some of your fellow Christians in a similar manner. Then see if you can draw upon the assistance of . . .

b. A visitation team

> The next day Peter started out with [the men Cornelius sent], and some of the brothers from Joppa went along. (10:23)

Peter did not go alone. Other believers made the trip with him. They were a team. Evangelism Explosion is a team visitation ministry that God has used to lead many thousands of seeking people to Christ. You may want to consider taking EE yourself, drawing on fellow believers to help you call on and witness to your non-Christian friends.

Another "must" if you are serious about helping searching people find Jesus Christ is . . .

c. A clear-cut gospel presentation

Then Peter began to speak. "I now realize how true it is that God does not show favoritism but accepts men from every nation who fear him and do what is right. You know the message God sent to the people of Israel, telling the good news of peace through Jesus Christ, who is Lord of all. You know what has happened throughout Judea, beginning in Galilee after the baptism that John preached—how God anointed Jesus of Nazareth with the Holy Spirit and power, and how he went around doing good and healing all who were under the power of the devil, because God was with him.

"We are witnesses of everything he did in the country of the Jews and in Jerusalem. They killed him by hanging him on a tree, but God raised him from the dead on the third day and caused him to be seen. He was not seen by all the people, but by witnesses whom God had already chosen—by us who ate and drank with him after he rose from the dead. He commanded us to preach to the people and to testify that he is the one whom God appointed as judge of the living and the dead. All the prophets testify about him that everyone who believes in him receives forgiveness of sins through his name." (10:34-43)

Notice how clearly, how concisely Peter shared the gospel with Cornelius' household. If you are not personally able to lead someone to Christ, you may want to ask a friend who is trained in EE to help you.

A young woman in our congregation began to develop a friendship with Jason. Jason, you may recall, was the bodybuilder mentioned in chapter seven. But Jason didn't know Christ. In fact, he mentioned to his friend in our church that he wished he knew that he was going to heaven.

The young woman didn't know exactly how to witness to him, so she invited Jack, an EE-trained elder from our church, *and Jason* over for the evening. Before the evening was over, Jason had found eternal life through Jesus Christ!

Some consider Evangelism Explosion too

"canned." They dislike its structured outline, its memorized verses and its well-prepared illustrations. They'd rather just open their mouth and let the Holy Spirit fill it.

Beth, whom I referred to in my earlier *Evangelism by the Book*, at first had this impression regarding EE. Then God used a very dramatic experience to open her eyes to the fact that she needed a structured gospel presentation.

"As I drove home from my first nervous presentation of the gospel," Beth said, "I told the Lord I was going to quit EE. Never mind that the woman whom I shared the gospel with had asked Jesus into her heart in spite of my stumbling delivery.

"I was busy convincing myself I didn't need a memorized, 'canned' outline to share the gospel. I'd been a Christian for 20 years. If God wanted me to witness, people would ask me about my faith and God would give me the words. Period.

"As I calmed down, I prayed, 'Lord, You know how I feel. If You really did tell me to be in EE and You want me to continue, You're going to have to give me the motivation, because I can't do it without You.'

"The words were barely framed when two blocks in front of me a pick-up skidded across the road and hit a telephone pole.

"I pulled into a parking place near the crash and got out of my car to see if I could help. I'm a respiratory therapist and teach cardiopulmonary resuscitation—CPR—as part of my job.

"Several motorists had pulled the man from the truck, but no one was doing anything more. I pushed through the crowd and knelt beside the victim. As I talked with him, I quickly located the pulse at his wrist. Questioning him about his pain, I noted the pulse under my fingers remained palpable but weak.

"As the moments ticked by, mechanically in my mind I reviewed the steps of CPR so that if the man was bleeding internally and should lose his pulse, I could immediately begin resuscitation without a moment's hesitation.

"The heartbeat continued. Paramedics arrived and took the injured man to the hospital. Back in my car, I was elated that the accident victim had lived. I thought back to my CPR training and how tiring it had been to learn each step and how we went over and over the same routines until they were second nature. But it was worth it! I could have performed CPR at that crash site almost instantly.

"Suddenly, I realized my prayer for motivation had been answered. The memorized and often-practiced EE outline was really no different from memorizing and practicing CPR over and over. With CPR I was ready to save a life anytime I was needed. With EE, I was equipped through the Holy Spirit's power to save a soul for eternity."

There are a number of very effective presentations that can be mastered. I especially like

EE. It will equip you to share Christ at a moment's notice with anyone you meet. But whatever method you choose, don't be caught unprepared to share your faith when you meet a person who is seeking Christ Jesus.

This chapter would be incomplete and inadequate if I did not mention the greatest Helper of all:

d. The Holy Spirit

> While Peter was still speaking these words, the Holy Spirit came on all who heard the message. (10:44)

Without the Holy Spirit your efforts and mine to witness are but vain salesmanship—zealous and well-meant, but fruitless human manipulation. Remember, you are not *dialogu*ing but "*trialoguing*"! Three persons are needed for dynamic, effective witnessing: the seeking sinner, the obedient messenger and the all powerful, all loving Holy Spirit! So whatever you do, be sure to submit yourself to the supreme control and sweetening influences of God's Spirit. He will attend your witness with power, conviction, love and fruitfulness.

Discussion Questions

1. Talk over this statement: "There are more people seeking after God than there are Christians helping them find Him." Why do

you think more Christians aren't involved in helping seeking people find God?

2. Why is it, all things being equal, that no one can reach your non-Christian "FRAN" better than you?

3. What are some of the most common hang-ups or obstacles that keep Christians from sharing their faith? What suggestions would you offer to help these believers over their hang-ups?

4. What is your church doing to make visitors feel loved and welcome? What are you doing or what might you do to use your home to reach out to your non-Christian friends and neighbors?

5. Do you have a clear-cut, always ready gospel presentation to share with someone when God opens the door of opportunity?

6. Describe your relationship to God's Holy Spirit. Is He in control? Does He empower you for witness?

Chapter Nine

Reflecting Christ in Your Life

John 9

J UDY SAW IN HER SISTER something new! There was a new gleam, a new life-style, a new value system. And this provoked in Judy's heart a very important question: "What brought about the change?" Then one day Judy saw Billy Graham on television and she discovered the answer. Her sister had trusted Christ for eternal life! She had experienced a miracle of God's grace in her heart! The *what* question suddenly became a *who* question. It was a Person—Jesus Christ—who brought about the notable change in her sister! And right then and there Judy, too, experienced the same transformation in her life!

When Christ enters a person's life, the changes He makes will cause others to ask what happened.

The account of the man blind from birth to whom Jesus gave the gift of sight (John 9) is a perfect case in point. As Jesus and His disciples left the temple grounds, they "saw a man blind from birth" (9:1). His condition sparked intellectual curiosity in Jesus' disciples. "Rabbi," they asked, "who sinned, this man or his parents, that he was born blind?" (9:2).

"Neither," was Jesus' reply. "This happened so that the work of God might be displayed in his life" (9:3). Christ's disciples saw in the man a theological problem. Jesus saw in him an opportunity for compassion. With His searching eye, He looked into his heart. Then He considered what He might make of the man. As a potter examines clay for fitness, so Jesus looked on this man and found the material to be good for displaying His glory.

What was the "work" Jesus had to do? He demonstrated it to His disciples. First, He opened the blind man's eyes. Next, He saved and transformed him. Then He elicited his devotion and worship. Finally, He sent him back to his family, friends and neighbors as a witness and a reflector of the Light which had transformed his life.

Jesus' miraculous healing, saving ministry to the man born blind is a lesson-packed parable for us today. I see four ways that you, having

come to Christ the saving Light, can reflect Him
to the lost people you love. The first way is by . . .

1. Your life

Christ's opening of the blind man's eyes
resembles His transforming work when He
saved you. Genuine conversion can no more be
hidden than a burning candle in a dark room.
Believers reflect Christ's light. They display the
work of God in their everyday life. Notice
some of the similarities between believers and
the blind man.

a. They were born "blind" and "begging."

> His disciples asked him, "Rabbi,
> who sinned, this man or his parents,
> that he was born blind?" . . .
> His neighbors and those who had
> formerly seen him begging asked,
> "Isn't this the same man who used to
> sit and beg?" (9:2, 8)

The affliction of blindness in that era had
rendered the man unable to earn a livelihood.
He was reduced to begging. He was a symbol
of all who are "dead in . . . transgressions and
sins" (Ephesians 2:1). "The god of this age has
blinded [their] minds . . . so that they cannot
see the light of the gospel of the glory of Christ,
who is the image of God" (2 Corinthians 4:4).
Having eyes, they see not. They are helpless
paupers, unable to free themselves from their

predicament. Not until Christ, the Light, in His mercy comes along and . . .

b. They are changed by Christ's miracle.

> [Jesus] spit on the ground, made some mud with the saliva, and put it on the man's eyes. "Go," he told him, "wash in the Pool of Siloam" (this word means Sent). So the man went and washed, and came home seeing. (John 9:6-7)

Christ's changing of the man's physical condition points for all time to His power to open the eyes of the spiritually blind. He alone can recreate in people the faculties sin has destroyed. Like the miracle of healing, salvation is beyond human power.

The saliva and the clay remind us of the gospel. How offensive is saliva and clay! And how people of the world sneer in disgust at a crucified Christ, as though He had any power to help! To Jews, Paul says, Christ crucified is "a stumbling block," and to Gentiles "foolishness." "But to those whom God has called, both Jews and Greeks, Christ [is] the power of God and the wisdom of God" (1 Corinthians 1:23-24).

Never forget from whose mouth the saliva came, or from whose wounds and death the gospel came! By that gospel harlots have been made chaste, thieves made honest, drunkards made sober. And by the power of that gospel your life has been gloriously changed. Then notice also . . .

c. Their "washing" led to their seeing.

To obtain physical sight the blind man had to exercise simple faith and wash in the pool of Siloam. His obedience opened to him a whole new world which he had never before seen! Likewise, all who would receive the gift of spiritual sight must wash in the cleansing blood that comes from the crucified Christ. And that spiritual cleansing leads amazingly to the discovery of a whole new spiritual world.

There is a mystical significance in the Pool of Siloam to which Jesus sent the blind man. It was not a cistern but a pool supplied by an underground channel from an overflowing spring. The earthly life of Jesus was much like the waters of that pool—visible, well-known, but with an overflowing source going back into eternity! The Jews could only see as far as Nazareth, Jesus' birthplace, and were offended at Him. But by simple faith, the blind man had his eyes opened to Christ's eternal origins! And then as with the healed blind man . . .

d. Their seeing leads to their witness.

His neighbors and those who had formerly seen him begging asked, "Isn't this the same man who used to sit and beg?" Some claimed that he was.

Others said, "No, he only looks like
him."

But he himself insisted, "I am the
man.".

"How then were your eyes
opened?" they demanded.

He replied, "The man they call Jesus
made some mud and put it on my
eyes. He told me to go to Siloam and
wash. So I went and washed, and then
I could see." (9:8-11)

Healed of his blindness, the man probably
returned to the spot of his healing. Not finding
Jesus there, he hurried home to tell his friends,
family and neighbors. And when asked by
them how it all happened, he pointed to "the
man they call Jesus."

As soon as the former blind man received his
sight, Jesus came to the forefront of his life.
Jesus became the most important Person in his
life. And his testimony was all about Jesus.
There was no uncertain sound; it was all Jesus!
With you it must be the same! When people
ask you how your life was so dramatically
changed, you too must be ready not only to
reflect Him in your life but to clearly tell about
Him with your lips.

Rod was born and raised in an unchurched
family. His dad, Harold, liked to hunt and to
take his sons Rod and Butch hunting on Sunday. Rod met and married Deb who, six years

after their marriage, was led to Christ by her aunt. Deb attended a rather legalistic church that didn't care for Rod and drove a wedge between the couple. This turned Rod, who thought he lived a pretty clean life, against the church.

Three years after Deb came to Christ some very traumatic events took place in Rod and Deb's lives. First, Harold divorced Rod's mother and moved to a town 40 miles north of Omaha, where he became deputy sheriff. One day he brought his guns down and asked Rod to put them in his house. Then he hired his other son, Butch, to burn down his house so he could collect insurance. When the authorities investigated the case, Harold said someone stole his guns and burned the house down. The only problem was that his son Rod had the guns, and the authorities found that out.

As time passed the authorities were suspicious that Harold and Butch had collaborated on the arson. Rod had to testify in court about the guns, and his father and brother were found guilty. Shortly after, Rod's father shot and killed both Rod's stepmother and himself.

Rod became very despondent. His testimony against his dad had led to his father's conviction and to the homicide-suicide of his stepmother and father. Rod's despondency threatened his own marriage. But about that time Deb's mom came from Oregon and invited the couple to attend a Saturday night outreach movie at our church. Rod was deeply moved by the movie. When Deb's aunt invited the couple to attend our worship service the next morning Rod agreed to go. The next Saturday night Rod and Deb were at a party, but Rod asked if they could leave and return to the church for another movie. That night *The Prodigal Son* was showing. At the end of the film, Pastor Bob made a statement that fit Rod like a glove.

"Sometimes," Pastor Bob said, "you have to go so low that only God can get you back up." Rod could not erase the pastor's words from his mind.

The next week I took an EE team to visit Rod and Deb in their home. Rod was ready. In fact, he was like ripened fruit waiting to be picked. The change in Rod's life was immediate and dramatic. Clarence, one of my teammates that night, took Rod under his wing and discipled him. Rod and Deb went through our New Beginnings class and became members of Christ Community Church. And not too long after that both Rod and Deb took our evangelism training.

They have since been on one of our mission trips to Antigua. They personally have led a number of people to Christ. Their two older children, Eric and Jaimee, have also become involved in EE and have taken several short-term mission trips. Eric feels called to missionary or pastoral ministry and is now enrolled at Grace

College of the Bible.

Jesus changed Rod's life. He and his whole family have become active witnesses for Christ!

2. Your lips

If you have been hesitant to speak out for Christ, the action of the former blind man should encourage you to do so.

The man's friends and neighbors saw in the sighted person before them a similarity to the blind man they knew, but they hesitated to admit that he was the same person. "But he himself insisted, 'I am the man.' " (9:9).

Sometimes people think they must memorize a perfect gospel presentation before they can lead a person to Christ. While you should do your best to be well prepared, sometimes to show His power and to receive the glory and praise due Him, God uses frail and imperfect efforts to witness. The important thing is to do your best!

Sonya is a good example. Sonya and Mario, her husband, are from El Salvador. Mario enrolled in EE at a church in Fulton, New York. But after a few weeks of study he had a job transfer to North Carolina. In class he had picked up some *Do You Know for Sure?* EE tracts. Before taking off for North Carolina, he left these on the bedroom dresser. Sonya found them, read the message carefully and decided she could use the tract to witness to her family.

She got on the phone and started calling long distance to various family members. Using the tract, she led one after another to Christ.

Of course Mario was excited to return home and find his wife already involved in friendship evangelism! They both praised God for using Sonya's simple gospel witness.

In the spiritual realm . . .

a. Miracles lead to questions.

> Those who had formerly seen [the blind man] begging asked, "Isn't this the same man who used to sit and beg?" . . . He . . . insisted, "I am the man."
>
> "How then were your eyes opened?" they demanded. (9:8-10)

Notice that first the people questioned the man's identity. But then they questioned the manner of his healing. They asked the "How?" question: "How then were your eyes opened?" How did this miracle come about?

Have people ever asked you about the change in your life?

Anna worked as a consultant. Over a period of a year she had talked by phone and built a friendly relationship with one of her clients, Bev. Although their contacts were only by telephone, Anna seemed somehow different—"positively so" to Bev. Bev's curiosity was piqued.

Anna was enrolled in EE, and she kept her EE

outline on her desk. Between phone calls to various clients, she studied the outline. One day as Anna was talking to Bev, Bev asked what kind of things Anna did between calls.

"I study EE," Anna responded. Bev, of course, wanted to know what EE was.

"We learn to ask people a couple of very interesting questions," Anna replied. Bev insisted that Anna ask her the questions.

So Anna began: "Bev, have you come to a place in your spiritual life where you can say you know for certain that if you were to die today you would go to heaven?"

"I don't think I can answer that," Bev responded. "Will you explain it to me?"

Actually, Anna was just in week two of her EE training and had only learned a very limited part of the gospel presentation. But she had her book in front of her, so she read the presentation to Bev over the phone. And right there on the phone Anna had the joy of leading her friend to Christ.

That week Anna took her EE team 28 miles into the country to do a follow-up visit with Bev, whom she had not met face to face before. And now Bev drives 56 miles round-trip every Sunday to worship with Anna at her church. Anna's may have not been the most perfect gospel presentation, but it was the very best she could do at the time. And God used it for His glory and for Bev's salvation!

b. Questions demand an answer.

> Some claimed that he was [the man born blind].
> Others said, "No, he only looks like him."
> But he himself insisted, "I am the man." (9:9)

The debate over the identity of the healed man standing before them was settled quickly: "I am he!" the formerly sightless man said.

And when he was asked the "How?" question, he pointed them to Jesus. He stuck to the facts with no unnecessary embellishments. The best answer for the critics and the most convincing proof of Christianity is a transformed life. Remember also that . . .

c. Witnesses don't have to be attorneys.

> "Where is this man [Jesus]?" they asked him.
> "I don't know," he said.
> They brought to the Pharisees the man who had been blind. Now the day on which Jesus had made the mud and opened the man's eyes was a Sabbath. Therefore the Pharisees also asked him how he had received his sight. "He put mud on my eyes," the man replied, "and I washed, and

now I see."

Some of the Pharisees said, "This man is not from God, for he does not keep the Sabbath."

But others asked, "How can a sinner do such miraculous signs?" So they were divided.

Finally they turned again to the blind man, "What have you to say about him? It was your eyes he opened."

The man replied, "He is a prophet."

The Jews still did not believe that he had been blind and had received his sight until they sent for the man's parents. "Is this your son?" they asked. "Is this the one you say was born blind? How is it that now he can see?"

"We know he is our son," the parents answered, "and we know he was born blind. But how he can see now, or who opened his eyes, we don't know. Ask him. He is of age; he will speak for himself." His parents said this because they were afraid of the Jews, for already the Jews had decided that anyone who acknowledged that Jesus was the Christ would be put out of the synagogue. That was why his parents said, "He is of age; ask him."

A second time they summoned the man who had been blind. "Give glory to God," they said. "We know this man is a sinner."

He replied, "Whether he is a sinner or not, I don't know. One thing I do know. I was blind but now I see!"

Then they asked him, "What did he do to you? How did he open your eyes?" (9:12-26)

The formerly blind man could not explain the miracle. But an explanation was not really needed. All that was needed was a testimony to the before and after of his experience: "One thing I do know. I was blind but now I see!" How often an unlettered believer sees what learned rabbis, doctors of the law and church synods totally miss. The plain and consistent testimony of the healed man triumphed over the critics' logic. In fact, it was when he began to argue and reason (9:27-34) that he got into trouble. It is wise to avoid argument at all times.

Tom and Denise went to southern Missouri for a week's vacation. While there they attended an Andy Williams concert. Before the concert, one of Andy's team came into the lobby to visit with the guests and to find out if they had any questions they wanted to ask Andy. Tom, always looking for an opportunity, volunteered two questions—EE's standard diagnostic questions! To Tom's surprise, when Andy had a break in his concert, he volunteered an answer to both questions. And both answers were unsatisfactory.

Arriving back in Omaha, Tom walked into a bowling alley to deliver some lighting fixtures for his company. The 46-year-old bowling alley owner asked, "What are those two question marks on your collar?"

"Oh, these?" Tom responded. "They're two questions I asked Andy Williams last week at his concert." When the owner expressed increased curiosity about the questions, Tom explained, "They represent a couple of important personal questions that have to do with spiritual matters. Do you have a few minutes? I'd like to ask them to you."

"Sure," the owner replied. "Let's go into my office where we can talk."

When the owner stepped out of his office, he was a new creation in Christ. Yes, Tom delivered the lighting fixtures, but he also presented the life-changing gospel.

Next, notice your need to reflect Christ by . . .

3. Your love

Christ's influence upon the family of the former blind man is an example of how you might reach your loved ones. Notice that the healed man exerted a witness to four groups of people with whom he had a relationship. Likewise you must . . .

a. Love your neighbors.

> His neighbors and those who had formerly seen him begging asked, "Isn't this the same man who used to sit and beg?" (9:8)

Notice from the longer Bible quotation just above how the healed man reflected Christ to his neighbors. What kind of witness are you developing with your neighbors?

This past Christmas I decided that my wife and I didn't know our neighbors well enough. So Donna prepared some goodies and wrapped them up as Christmas gifts. Then, armed with the gifts and several invitations to our church's Christmas celebration, Donna and I visited each of our neighbors two doors in each direction on both sides of the street. We have continued to pray for them personally and are working hard to develop a witness to each of them.

Do you know your neighbors? Are you building a loving relationship with them? In your outreach you need also to . . .

b. Love your associates.

> Those who had formerly seen him begging asked, "Isn't this the same man who used to sit and beg?" (9:8)

This verse suggests the newly sighted man

also had a witness to his associates—people with whom he had contact on a regular basis. How is your witness to your associates?

For several years I have tried to go regularly to the same barber so that I can build a warm relationship with and witness to her. I have also sought to reach out to the young man who services my IRA plan. How about you? Do you need to broaden your witness to include all the people with whom you regularly associate? Do you pray that God will give you opportunity to present Christ to them?

Fred had been going to the same barber for 20 years. With love he had reached out to him in many ways, building a trust relationship. One Friday evening the barber came to Fred's basement door. Fred could see that the man was in great emotional distress.

Fred invited him in and listened with empathy as the barber confessed that his marriage was falling apart. After some time of listening and counseling, Fred had the joy of leading his barber to Christ.

Vic is field superintendent for Fred's heating and air-conditioning business. Twenty-four years ago he started as an apprentice. Fred could see at that time that Vic had a lot of potential. As they worked together Fred built a trust relationship with Vic. He invited Vic and Carol to a Christian Businessman's dinner and exposed them to the gospel in many other ways. But they didn't seem to see their need for

Christ until their marriage began to unravel. Vic especially feared for the future of his two small children. In Fred's office, the two men talked at length. Fred lovingly warned Vic that the price to his family would be high if he didn't let Christ straighten out his life. At last, Vic prayed to receive Christ into his heart. Today he is a committed Christian layman. Best of all, his two children, one in high school and the other in college, still have the same parents!

That brings me naturally to your need to . . .

c. Love your family.

> The Jews still did not believe that he had been blind and had received his sight until they sent for the man's parents. "Is this your son?" they asked. "Is this the one you say was born blind?" (9:18-19)

At the beginning of this chapter I shared with you how Judy had been influenced for Christ by her sister. How very many people have come to Christ through family members! What are you doing to have a witness to those whom you love the most: parents, grandparents, spouse, brothers, sisters, children, grandchildren?

When Whitney was just seven years old, she asked her father, Fred, how to "get Jesus into my heart." Fred tried to explained sin to her and how Jesus wanted her to have a clean heart that He could live in.

Whitney wasn't sure she had sinned, so Fred asked her if she had ever told a lie. She admitted she had told quite a few. Patiently Fred helped her understand that she needed to confess her sins and invite Jesus into her life. A month later, just before she was baptized, Whitney told the whole church how Jesus had come into her heart.

A year later, when Whitney was eight, Fred overheard her telling her friend Megan that she needed Jesus in her heart and explaining how to invite Him in. Today, Whitney is a grown woman and works as a volunteer in the local hospital. Recently a patient confessed to her that she was afraid of death.

"Afraid?" Whitney asked. "You just need to invite Jesus into your heart. When He comes in as your Savior He will give you His peace and eternal life."

Recently Fred's son, Marshall, was over for dinner with his new wife, Vickie. Vickie was celebrating because she had just led her 20-year-old nephew to the Lord. Fred is rejoicing that his family, one by one, is coming to Christ and that they, in turn, are leading others in their network of relations to Christ!

But the Bible teaches that you should also . . .

d. Love your adversaries.

A second time they summoned the man who had been blind. "Give glory to God," they said. "We know this man is a sinner."

He replied, "Whether he is a sinner or not, I don't know. One thing I do know. I was blind but now I see!"

Then they asked him, "What did he do to you? How did he open your eyes?"

He answered, "I have told you already and you did not listen. Why do you want to hear it again? Do you want to become his disciples, too?"

Then they hurled insults at him and said, "You are this fellow's disciple! We are disciples of Moses! We know that God spoke to Moses, but as for this fellow, we don't even know where he comes from."

The man answered, "Now that is remarkable! You don't know where he comes from, yet he opened my eyes. We know that God does not listen to sinners. He listens to the godly man who does his will. Nobody has ever heard of opening the eyes of a man born blind. If this man were not from God, he could do nothing."

To this they replied. "You were steeped in sin at birth; how dare you lecture us!" And they threw him out. (9:24-34)

It is obvious that the former blind man did everything he could to persuade even his adversaries that Jesus was the Son of God, the true Messiah. He wanted them to become Christ's disciples too.

One day Mel, a state and national wrestling champion with a neck as thick as a small tree trunk, noticed that his neighbor had dumped his garbage on Mel's lawn. At first, Mel was greatly agitated. But he waited awhile until he had prayed at length about the matter. Then he went over to talk with his neighbor.

Mel never brought up the matter of the garbage. Instead, he asked his neighbor about his spiritual condition. To Mel's great surprise, the neighbor opened up to the gospel and prayed to receive Christ into his heart!

Finally, you can reflect Christ by passing on to others His light, which by faith has now become . . .

4. Your light

As Christ gave physical light to the blind man, so you have been commissioned to bring spiritual light to lost people. But God does not expect you to do it all by yourself. You must be sure to . . .

a. Mobilize new believers.

While the conversion experience is fresh in their hearts, while they still have many unbelieving friends, neighbors and relatives, while their zeal and enthusiasm is still high, help the newly born-again to witness. You personally can go with them to witness. You can encourage them to take evangelism training. You can suggest they bring their non-churched friends and family to your house of worship. Enlist them while the window of opportunity is open.

Julie is a very active witness and discipler today. But two years ago she didn't have a clue about Christ or Christianity. She had no religious background and wasn't interested! Not interested, that is, until she met Barbie, whom she had known back in third grade. The two hadn't seen each other for years. Then suddenly the two met in their environmental geology class at the University of Nebraska in Omaha.

Barbie invited Julie to a Zeta Chi costume party at her home. That night a blizzard made it impossible for Julie to go home, so she spent the night at Barbie's and they stayed up late talking. When she awakened early the next morning, she found a Bible on the coffee table and began reading it. Over the next six months Barbie and Julie began seeing a lot of each other. Each time they would meet, Barbie shared bits of her testimony or the gospel.

When Christmas approached, Barbie invited Julie to our Christmas musical, then to "Night Life," a Sunday evening college group which discussed subjects like dating. That night Julie went home, went into her bedroom and asked Jesus to come into her life.

For follow-up Barbie invited another friend, Rene, to join Julie and her for a weekly Bible study. But before long Julie was off to Mexico on an intensive Spanish language course and then she was into an English language teaching program. Without her close Christian friends to nurture her, Julie began to flounder spiritually. She began to have some doubts about the Bible. No one was there to answer her questions.

At last she returned to Omaha and, as she explained it, "The Holy Spirit took hold of my life and changed and motivated me very much." An opportunity opened for Julie to move into an apartment with four other college girls—all Christians. Then Barbie's Aunt Julie began to disciple Julie on Saturday mornings and enlisted her for EE training.

"I loved EE training," Julie says. "True, I struggled a bit with the outline, but it gives me a structured, logical way to share the gospel."

One evening Julie was asked to pick up a Chinese student, June Li, and take her to church. Afterwards Julie told June she was starting a daily Bible study and invited her to join it. For the first lesson, Julie decided to share an extended EE presentation. That evening June Li prayed to receive Christ. She has been coming to international Sunday school and to the worship services and growing rapidly in the Lord.

Giving an African student a ride to lunch, Julie led him to Christ. Julie's brother, Kennedy, started coming to various college activities at the church and then attended a retreat where he saw Julie baptized. Shortly after that, following the church's student prayer meeting, Julie asked Kennedy the two diagnostic questions, explained the gospel to him and led her brother to Christ. Now the two of them are praying for their parents, who, noticing the unusual change in their daughter and son, have started attending Christ Community Church.

New believers, like lambs, need abundant tender care. They need nurture. But they also need to lead others to Christ and become active in reaching their friends and family for Christ! That's the discipling process that Christ modeled and mandated for His followers.

b. Expect some rejection.

> Jesus said, "For judgment I have come into this world, so that the blind will see and those who see will become blind.
>
> Some Pharisees who were with him heard him say this and asked, "What? Are we blind too?"
>
> Jesus said, "If you were blind, you would not be guilty of sin; but now that you claim you can see, your guilt

remains." (9:39-41)

The Pharisees were so firmly in the grip of darkness that they only saw what they interpreted to be Jesus' small breach in their law. They totally missed the spectacular, miraculous triumph of light over darkness.

Jesus warns elsewhere: "This is the verdict: Light has come into the world, but men loved darkness instead of light because their deeds were evil. Everyone who does evil hates the light, and will not come into the light for fear that his deeds will be exposed." (John 3:19-20).

Actually, people in darkness don't reject you, the witness. They reject Christ, the true Light.

c. Help new believers to worship.

> Jesus . . . said, "Do you believe in the Son of Man?"
>
> "Who is he, sir?" the [former blind] man asked. "Tell me so that I may believe in him."
>
> Jesus said, "You have now seen him; in fact, he is the one speaking with you."
>
> Then the man said, "Lord, I believe," and he worshiped him. (9:35-38)

What a fitting conclusion to this man's encounter with Christ! At first Christ to him was a "man" (9:11); then he saw Christ as a "prophet" (9:17); then as the *Son of Man* (9:35); and finally he worshiped Him as "Lord" (9:38)! What a beautiful close to the man's encounter with the true Light of the world! Enlightened both physically and spiritually, he prostrated himself in adoring gratitude at the feet of his Savior, the Sun of Righteousness. In the same way, you and I must help new believers to grow in their knowledge of Christ and to express their faith in regular worship.

The last lesson I share from this miracle event has to do with the crucial element of time. In reflecting Christ the Light to others you must . . .

d. Shine while it is day.

> Said Jesus, . . . "As long as it is day, we must do the work of him who sent me. Night is coming, when no one can work. While I am in the world, I am the light of the world." (9:3-5)

The sun was possibly going down over the holy city when Jesus and His disciples saw the man born blind. By Jewish reckoning, it was the Sabbath, but Jesus would not postpone for another 24 hours the important work of healing and saving this needy man. He would risk the Pharisees' animosity rather then fail to do God's work.

Occasions for sharing God's saving grace come your way every day. Will you see them and promptly respond? Or will you ignore these golden opportunities?

There are limits that you need to be sensitive to. Lengthening shadows are a reminder of the shortness of time. Neighbors move away. Associates have job transfers. Family members pass away. Friends suddenly drop out of your life.

You need to develop accountability and a scheduled plan for building rapport with those whom God expects you to win to Christ. If you leave your witness to the spur of the moment or to some favorable turn of events, the opportunity may never come.

I suggest again that you look over the *Six-Step Approach to Friendship Evangelism* in the back of this book. You may use it to chart your relational evangelism over a one-year period with at least one person—friend, relative, associate or neighbor.

A family of four moved into the house behind Charlie and Grace. The husband, David, was an attorney. His wife, Karen, was a nutritionist. While they were moving in, Grace fixed a whole meal for the family. Charlie and Grace cultivated the relationship in every way possible. They had David and Karen and their two daughters over for a barbecue. They kept house for them when they were away on trips.

After the relationship was solid, Charlie and Grace invited their neighbors to church. During the communion service both David and

Karen committed their lives to Christ. Today David is a deeply committed elder in that church and Karen is a deaconess. Now they, in turn, are demonstrating the same concern to build relationships with their neighbors and friends. They are reflecting the same unconditional love and care which Charlie and Grace extended to them.

Discussion Questions

1. Why do you think a changed life is such an important witness to non-Christians? Can you think of someone whose changed life God is using as a testimony of His saving grace?

2. Why should you not argue with non-Christians? What is the difference between testifying and arguing?

3. Who particularly did the blind man witness to? What is the significance of his witnessing to these people? Might you be called sometime to witness to adversaries?

4. Why do you think it is wise to help new believers begin witnessing to their friends as soon as possible?

5. What progression took place in the blind man's understanding of who Christ is? What spiritual exercise or discipline did the blind man's healing and conversion lead to?

6. What does John 9:4—"As long as it is day, we must do the work of him who sent me. Night is coming, when no man can work"—mean to you? How should it affect your witness?

Chapter Ten

Crowding People to Christ

Luke 19:1-10

N OTHING IS SO uncertain and unpredictable as a crowd," remarked Livy, the noted Roman historian, in 29 B.C.

Livy's comment is still true! Calm, orderly and indifferent, in a matter of seconds a crowd can be moved to laugh, cry, applaud, praise, deride, threaten or even profane. The same throng has been known to challenge and cheer, to jostle and jeer, to hoot and harangue, to degrade and destroy and finally to crush and kill.

This fickle phenomenon prompted Thomas Fuller to remark, "The mob has many heads but no brains," and Emerson to add, "The mob is a man voluntarily descending to the nature of a beast."

But it needs to be added that although a crowd at times can be deviating, distrustful and dangerous, in the hands of an effective leader it can be a force for good. As someone quipped, "Every crowd may have its silver lining." Such was the crowd that surrounded Jesus as He passed through Jericho:

> Jesus entered Jericho and was passing through. A man was there by the name of Zacchaeus; he was a chief tax collector and was wealthy. He wanted to see who Jesus was, but being a short man he could not, because of the crowd. So he ran ahead and climbed a sycamore-fig tree to see him, since Jesus was coming that way.
>
> When Jesus reached the spot, he looked up and said to him, "Zacchaeus, come down immediately. I must stay at your house today." So he came down at once and welcomed him gladly.
>
> All the people saw this and began to mutter, "He has gone to be the guest of a 'sinner.' "
>
> But Zacchaeus stood up and said to the Lord, "Look, Lord! Here and now I give half of my possessions to the poor, and if I have cheated anybody out of anything, I will pay back four times the amount."

> Jesus said to him, "Today salvation has come to this house, because this man, too, is a son of Abraham. For the Son of Man came to seek and to save what was lost." (Luke 19:1-10)

As Jesus passed through Jericho seeking to save the lost, He drew a large crowd. He had worked many miracles and His fame had spread far and wide. In that crowd was a tax collector, utterly despised by those around him. But deep within his being was an unmet need. He was thirsty for the water of life. He sensed that somehow Jesus could meet his need. But Zacchaeus was a short man and the crowd was large. He didn't have much chance to even get a glimpse of Jesus, much less talk to Him.

But where there's a will there's a way. Zacchaeus ran on ahead and found a tree in which he could perch and enjoy a full view of the Savior as He passed by. Only Jesus didn't pass by! He stopped and made an appointment to visit the little tax collector in his home. And by the end of the visit, Jesus could announce, "Today salvation has come to this house"!

Notice that in His encounter with Zacchaeus, Jesus gave a concise statement of His life purpose on earth and His objective for visiting Jericho: "The Son of man came to seek and to save what was lost" (19:10). Clearly, God had used a crowd to draw a seeking sinner to the Savior.

The church needs to use its crowds creatively to bring individuals to Christ. Yes, people are won to Christ through one-to-one contact. But friendship evangelism extends to the crowds, too. People are drawn to Christ at camp meetings, large evangelistic crusades, youth conferences, ski retreats, Easter musicals, Friendship Sundays, tent revivals—wherever a throng of people is gathered for the purpose of introducing non-Christians to the Savior.

I want to take a closer look at Zacchaeus and notice in that short-of-stature Jewish tax collector four characteristics commonly found in people who gather in crowds. First, like Zacchaeus, people are . . .

1. Crowding

What is it about a crowd that God uses for His eternal purposes? What good can come out of such a mass of uncontrollable humanity?

a. People naturally follow a crowd.

Curiosity, probably more than anything else, attracted that crowd in Jericho. Curiosity is an endowment that prompts us humans to thrust our noses into everything, even things that don't concern us. Everyone is born with an inquisitive eagerness to see and hear that which is attracting the interest of others—especially large numbers of others.

Lord Chesterfield in his *Letters to His Son* commented, "Observe any meeting of people, and you will always find their eagerness and impetuosity rise or fall in proportion to their numbers." Large numbers of people create large portions of curiosity. That curiosity, in turn, draws people almost beyond their control.

I was teaching an Evangelism Explosion Leadership Training Clinic in Walden, New York. About half way through the clinic, one of the pastors locked his keys in his car. Fortunately, there was a Chevrolet dealer next door to the church. So the pastor asked a mechanic to come over and open his car door. In the course of conversation, the mechanic asked, "What are all these cars doing here today? This isn't Sunday. What is going on?"

The pastor, very alert, replied, "It's a very interesting gathering of people. But look, you need to get back to the garage and I need to get back to class. Do you have a little time after work? We could meet here at my car and I'll tell you all about what's going on."

Out of curiosity the mechanic was back at 5 o'clock that day. The pastor not only explained to him the clinic, but he had the joy of using his EE training to lead the mechanic to Christ!

The wise pastor, evangelist or lay person who wants to reach people for Christ will capitalize on this curiosity to reach out to his or her friends, family and neighbors. Many people who avoid personal one-to-one encounters will accept an invitation to join a crowd. Perhaps this is because . . .

b.   Individuals can get lost in a crowd.

Picture in your mind for a moment short Zacchaeus getting swallowed up in that crowd. Keeping his elbows close to his body, he goes one way and then another, trying to squeeze to the center of things. But the press of humanity is too dense. He stands on tiptoes, hoping to glimpse the action. But all he sees are impenetrable shoulders.

While there is some discomfort in a crowd, there may be safety in numbers. People like the anonymity. It is nonthreatening. The speaker is looking at everyone and singling out no one. His or her message is directed at the whole gathering.

In the summer of 1942, nine-year-old Tommy watched as his older brothers and sisters walked up the Nyack College hillside to join the large gathering of young people in the college chapel. Tommy's curiosity got the better of him, and he asked his mom to take him to the youth meeting. Since neither mother nor son qualified as "youth," they had to sit in the balcony above the sea of youthful faces.

It is doubtful that the evangelist, Merv Rosell, even saw Tommy up in the balcony. But as he spoke, Tommy listened carefully and with deepening conviction. He was back the next night and the next. On the closing night of the conference Tommy walked down the hillside with his mother and went to bed. But he couldn't sleep. Deep conviction gripped him. He feared Jesus would come again or he would die without having put his trust in the Savior. Finally, at about midnight, he knocked on his mother's bedroom door and asked her to pray with him to receive Jesus.

I was that nine-year-old boy. I was sitting up in the balcony above the crowd just like Zacchaeus was in the tree above the Jericho crowd. Today I continue to be very thankful that Jesus singled me out of that crowd and brought salvation to me.

c. Crowds cannot hide from God.

The eyes of our ever-present God are watching every place. Nothing is hidden from Him! His Spirit penetrates even into the deepest and innermost places of our lives.

The crowd couldn't hide Zacchaeus from Jesus. The branches and leaves couldn't veil his face from the Savior. How wonderful that Jesus found the smallest, least conspicuous person in that large crowd and reached out to him with His salvation!

Al had come from Chicago to Omaha to supervise the construction of a new theater. One Thursday evening Denise, a member of Christ Community Church, met him and invited him to visit our church. Al didn't intend to come. In fact, at a bar the next evening he jokingly told some of his friends about the invitation.

"Don't laugh!" one of the men responded. "Have you seen how many cars are parked in their lot every Sunday? They must have something good happening there!"

Out of curiosity Al decided he would accept Denise's invitation and visit the church on Sunday. Denise had described Al to Carol, one of the regular greeters, so that she could recognize him and greet him by name. Sure enough, when Al arrived Carol recognized him and to his great surprise said, "Good morning. You must be Al!" Carol introduced him to an usher who seated Al next to a very friendly lady who made him feel welcome and helped him find hymns and the Scriptures.

Al was so moved by the music and message that tears ran down his cheeks. When Pastor Bob gave the invitation, Al prayed and trusted Christ as his Savior. So excited was he about his newfound faith that he started coming to every church activity he could squeeze in!

What was it that God used to draw Al to our church and ultimately to the Savior? Was it not the large number of cars in our parking lot and the crowds of interested people represented by those cars? Al thought he could get lost in that crowd, but our Savior, Who came to seek and save the lost, found Al hidden away in that Sunday morning crowd of worshipers.

The second way people resemble Zacchaeus is in their natural propensity for . . .

2. Collecting

We're told that Zacchaeus was a collector of taxes. In fact, he was the *chief* tax collector! Jericho was on the road from Peraea to Judea and Egypt. It was one of the largest taxation centers in Palestine. It had an important custom house, and Zacchaeus was the head of the customs department. Little wonder the people of Jericho had no use for Zacchaeus!

As I noted in an earlier chapter, the Romans subcontracted the collection of taxes in Palestine to local Jewish people. The Romans would assess a district a certain annual tax and award the collection contract to the highest bidder. The collector was free to charge people whatever he could, as long as he turned over the assessed amount at the end of the year. The surplus went into his pocket. Common people had no way of knowing how much was right, so the practice led to gross abuse.

With such a contract, Zacchaeus collected from his fellow countrymen poll taxes, ground taxes, income taxes, duties for using roads, market taxes, taxes on carts, taxes on a wide variety of other articles as well as import/export taxes. Like all other tax collectors of that day, Zacchaeus was classified along with robbers and murderers. He was barred from the synagogue. People despised him.

But people's opinions didn't matter to Zacchaeus. He was collecting for himself plenty of wealth! And, sad to say, many in our society today have the same attitude. Like Zacchaeus . . .

a. People spend a lifetime collecting things.

Everyone collects something. I collect elephants. No, not real live ones, but ceramic elephants from Vietnam, ivory elephants given to me from my mother-in-law, who was a missionary in Côte d'Ivoire, ebony elephants from Sri Lanka. I was given a key chain from Thailand with a brass elephant on it. You can't sit in my office very long without noticing my collection of elephants.

Some people collect baseball cards. Or coins. Or stamps. Or tea cups. Or spoons. Zacchaeus collected money. For Zacchaeus it wasn't a pastime. It was a passion!

Money and collectibles are, for the most part, amoral. Like fire, they can serve either good or evil purposes. But if they are not kept under control, they can become the strongest slaveholders in the world. They can be the cause of restless living and premature death. People are trying frantically to earn enough money to pay for the things they're too busy to enjoy. Like Zacchaeus, despite all their collecting, there is still a big void in their lives.

Paul remarked to Timothy, "We brought nothing into the world, and we can take nothing out of it. But if we have food and clothing, we will be content with that" (1 Timothy 6:7-8). Although certain basics are a legitimate quest, . . .

b. Collecting things can be sinful and harmful.

As I said, both money and things tend to be amoral. It is not money but the *love* of money that is sinful. Likewise with other possessions. In our insatiable desire for them lies the evil. In covetousness is the sin.

Probably a home and a car are the two objects which the average American male works hardest to secure. Someone observed that a man's first ambition is to own his own home and, second, to own a car to get away from his home! Then, of course, the home has to be furnished—comfortably so—and the car gassed and oiled and soon replaced. And so the rat race is on!

When it comes to money, it has been said that even a penny, if held close enough to the eye, will hide the biggest star in the sky. Love of money causes people to lose sight of eternal values, sell their souls and live lives of emptiness. For that reason, the rich young ruler went away from Christ sorrowful (Matthew 19:16-22).

Although money is the universal provider of almost everything, it can't buy happiness. Money is the universal passport to almost everywhere, but not to heaven! Whatever your station in life, you need to remember that . . .

c. Things and money ultimately don't satisfy.

Twenty centuries ago collecting money didn't

bring Zacchaeus much satisfaction. He still had a large vacuum in the center of his being which no amount of collecting could satisfy.

Some of the world's richest people have confessed the same dissatisfaction. John D. Rockefeller admitted, "I have made millions, but they have brought me no happiness." W.H. Vanderbilt wrote, "The care of 200 million dollars is too great a load for any brain or back to bear." John Jacob Astor complained, "I am the most miserable man on earth!" And Henry Ford admitted late in life, "I was happier when doing a mechanic's job."

Do I hear you saying, "I'll avoid covetousness and find happiness by giving it all away; I'll keep just enough to live comfortably"? Even that solution to the problem of collecting, while praiseworthy, isn't foolproof.

Andrew Carnegie, the great industrialist and philanthropist, gave away millions of dollars to schools, libraries and churches. In his retirement years he was bombarded daily by people who wanted a share of his wealth. To "help" him, a British syrup company ran a contest, "How Mr. Carnegie Should Get Rid of His Wealth." People submitted 45,000 suggestions! A fourth of them were personal requests for part of his fortune.

Carnegie discovered that it isn't easy to wisely, joyfully, systematically give away millions of dollars. He soon tired of distributing his wealth. "You have no idea the strain I have been under," he confided in a letter to a friend. In a speech delivered in Scotland, he departed from his prepared text to confess: "Millionaires who laugh are rare, very rare, indeed."

3. Climbing

Zacchaeus, knowing the crowd would block his view of Jesus, ran ahead of the crowd and climbed a sycamore-fig tree. What a picture of Zacchaeus' life! Zacchaeus had spent all his life trying to climb to the top. No doubt in school he had tried to reach the top of his class. In his community he probably tried to have the best home. In his occupation he did reach the top: he was a chief tax collector! But Zacchaeus couldn't do much about his stature. Being short, the only way to be at the top of that crowd of people was to climb a tree. Certainly Zacchaeus was resourceful!

Today, it is the same. . . .

a. People want to climb to the top.

For most people, life is a long struggle, conscious or unconscious, for advancement, promotion and success. It's an all-out effort to get as close as possible to the top of the ladder. And you will notice that in their efforts . . .

b. To reach the top, some people step on others.

Tax collectors, probably more than anyone else in Jewish society, got their wealth and made it to the top of their field by stepping on others. They cheated, lied, abused, stole, deceived, defrauded. To get ahead, they employed just about any other wicked practice ever devised. And all of it at the expense of others. They sacrificed character, reputation and self-worth for success, wealth and power. Little wonder that they were among the most hated scoundrels in the community! But having gone through that cutthroat struggle, they sadly discovered that . . .

c. The top doesn't usually satisfy.

Finding out that the top of the pile doesn't satisfy is no doubt what drove Zacchaeus to the top of the tree to see Jesus! Could this miracle-working Prophet from Nazareth somehow satisfy his inner craving?

In his book about famous people, Wayne Warner says of J.C. Penney: "[He] was a man of advanced years before he committed his life to Jesus Christ. He was a good man [and] honest, but primarily interested in becoming a success and making money."

Warner goes on to tell how one day Mrs. Penney caught cold, developed pneumonia and died. "When she died," Penney confessed, "my world crashed about me. To build a business, to be a success in the eyes of men, to accumulate money—that was the purpose of life?"

A series of other trials brought Penney financial ruin and deep distress of spirit. God was dealing with his self-righteous nature and his love for money. To make things worse, he fell ill and had to be hospitalized. In the hospital with no money even to pay for his care, he suddenly heard an old familiar song coming from the little chapel down the hall:

Be not dismayed whate'er betide,
    God will take care of you . . .

Penney slipped out of his room and made his way to the small chapel, finding a seat in the back.

"Lord," he prayed, "by myself I can do nothing. Will You take care of me?"

He testified that a weight lifted from off his spirit and he returned to his room a different man. He began to read the Bible. Restored to health, he became an active layman. He began to trust the Lord as he had never done before. It wasn't long before he had recovered his business losses.

The second part of Penney's long life was in every way better than the first. He found that coming to Jesus brought him true satisfaction.

Whether like J.C. Penney, among people in a small hospital chapel, or like Al, in a large worship service, God reaches out to meet the needs of individuals. And however small or large the crowd at such gospel gatherings, there are those who, in the footsteps of Zacchaeus, are . . .

4. Coming

Some may come out of curiosity, or from some other less-than-spiritual motive. But as with Al, once they come, the Holy Spirit has opportunity to work upon their minds and hearts. When these come they will find that . . .

a. Coming to Jesus brings true satisfaction.

Lisa not only had found no satisfaction in her life, but she was totally despondent and desperate. Her job was on the line, her relationships had fallen apart and she had no reason to keep on living. She didn't know where to turn.

Finally Lisa decided to end it all. She set out the various paraphernalia needed to destroy her life. All was in readiness. But just before she took the final fatal steps, she spotted a Bible that a friend had given her. *Before I do it,* she thought to herself, *maybe I should see what that Bible has to say.*

That decision postponed Lisa's dreadful plan until later. Meanwhile a friend invited her to go to church with her Sunday morning. At the worship service Lisa listened intently as Pastor Bob presented Christ Who alone can satisfy. At the end of the message Lisa invited Christ into her life.

Lisa couldn't believe the newfound joy that flooded her life. She became involved in a singles group at the church, she enlisted in evangelism training, she found a biblical purpose for living. Today, Lisa is another proof that God can and does speak to individuals in a crowd, meeting their deepest needs and giving them through Christ a satisfying, fulfilling life.

b. Only Jesus can change a sinner's heart.

How beautifully Christ changed Zacchaeus' heart! Zacchaeus took steps to show all the community that he was a changed man. He gave half of his wealth to the poor. With the other half he made restitution to the people he had cheated, going far beyond what Jewish law required. By the grace of Christ Jesus he was changed from a greedy miser to a generous giver, from one who used people to one who helped people. It's amazing how the person who comes to Christ gets a new attitude toward money—a new attitude that straightens out almost every other area of his or her life!

A young man, Brian, had sought satisfaction in drugs, night life and company with the wrong crowd. One day he traveled on his motorcycle from Nebraska to northwest Iowa. As he sped past the Okoboji Bible Conference grounds, something drew him toward the crowds in and around the large meeting place. He decided to turn around and investigate.

As he sat in the crowd that overflowed the building, Brian heard from God. God showed him he couldn't find satisfaction in his fast and furious night life. Like Zacchaeus, Brian came to Jesus and was transformed into a new person. Since then he has led scores of people to Christ. Today he is in seminary, planning to become a missionary to Russia.

c. Jesus came to save whole "households."

The story of Zacchaeus comes to a glorious conclusion on our theme of relational evangelism. Jesus came to Zacchaeus' *oikos*—his household!

How interesting that Jesus should say to him, "Today I must stay at your *house*"! Again we see the New Testament pattern. Jesus wants to follow the salvation of individuals with the salvation of their entire networks of friends, relatives, associates and neighbors.

Scott invited one of his customers, Kirk, to lunch. Over lunch Scott shared the good news of Christ and invited Kirk to a Christmas concert at Christ Community Church. Kirk gladly accepted the invitation and brought his wife and her parents to the concert. Sitting among the crowd of over 2,000 gathered that night, the four heard a brief presentation of the gospel. All four of them received Christ as their Savior. Then they began inviting other family members and friends to join them in the services at the church. Others in Kirk's *oikos* also came to Christ. His witness continues to permeate his "household."

The outreach ministry of our church has launched a ministry to enhance the friendship evangelism efforts of our people. We borrowed the idea from the Church Growth Institute, Lynchburg, Virginia. The institute calls the ministry "FRANtastic Days," FRAN being our acronym for *friends*, *relatives*, *associates*, *neighbors*. The goal of FRANtastic Sunday is a planned quarterly service—an Easter drama, a Christmas concert or a "visitor-friendly" event featuring a Christian celebrity—that God can use to speak to non-Christians in the crowded sanctuary.

At Christ Community Church we have seen our FRANtastic Sunday attendance jump from 2,300 to as high as 7,000 as our people invite their friends, relatives, associates and neighbors to a nonthreatening, enjoyable event climaxed by a brief but clear presentation of the gospel.

A young woman who attended our Easter FRANtastic service told our church congregation that she enjoyed it so much she came back for a second performance. And at the close of the second, she invited Christ into her life. Now she was confessing her faith by being baptized!

Is your church providing opportunities for people to "get lost" in a crowd—opportunities for God to speak to them in their moment of need? Are you availing yourself of such opportunities to invite your friends, relatives, associates and neighbors to meet the Savior Who came to seek and to save those who are lost?

Their motive for attending may be ulterior.

But the Holy Spirit of God is able to speak to them right there in the crowd. And, like Zacchaeus, salvation may come both to them and to their households!

Discussion Questions

1. What about a crowd attracts people? Is this good or bad? Explain.

2. What—or who—was the "silver lining" in the "crowd" that gathered in Jericho? What—or who—caused it to turn out as it did?

3. What was Jesus' life purpose as stated in this incident? How was it seen that day in Jericho?

4. How might the church use the phenomenon of crowds for redemptive purposes?

5. Why are some people more attracted to a crowd and more apt to respond in a crowd than in a one-to-one situation?

6. What do you think the best approach is to reach someone who all his life has been consumed by a passion to collect and climb?

7. What is the significance of Jesus' coming to Zacchaeus's "house" and of His statement, "Today salvation has come to this house"?

Chapter Eleven

Praying People to Christ

First Timothy 1:18-2:8

M Y GRANDFATHER, John Hartman, was a godly man, a fruitful missionary, a gifted teacher and a loving father. But somehow all of his children but one drifted into the world, married unbelievers and lived lives far from God. But Grandfather never gave up on them. He loved them unconditionally and prayed daily, fervently and expectantly for them.

Although he lived to be nearly 90, Grandpa Hartman didn't see his prayers answered during his lifetime. But at his funeral three of his children turned to Christ. Later the most prodigal of all—a son—was gloriously saved and became a fruitful witness to everyone around him.

God uses many different means to draw people to His Son, the Savior. Some people have turned to Jesus Christ at evangelistic banquets, others through a gospel message on TV or radio. For still others, it has been the influence of a salvation tract, an evangelistic crusade, a gospel film or a friend's personal witness.

In the previous chapter I focused on "crowding people to Christ"—public events deliberately arranged to create a climate where Christ can speak to them, as He did to Zacchaeus, out of the crowd. In this chapter I turn to First Timothy 1:18-2:8 in order to emphasize the importance of "praying people to Christ." The point I shall underscore is this: *God wants you to pray for the salvation of people—especially your FRANs.*

Look carefully at four important facets of this subject: (1) the PRIORITY of prayer, (2) the PATTERN for prayer, (3) the PEOPLE for whom you should pray and (4) the PLACES where you should pray.

1. The *priority* of prayer

> I urge, then, first of all, that requests, prayers, intercession and thanksgiving be made for everyone—for kings and all those in authority, that we may live peaceful and quiet lives in all godliness and holiness. This is good,

and pleases God our Savior, who wants all men to be saved and to come to a knowledge of the truth. For there is one God and one mediator between God and men, the man Christ Jesus, who gave himself as a ransom for all men—the testimony given in its proper time. And for this purpose I was appointed a herald and an apostle—I am telling the truth, I am not lying—and a teacher of the true faith to the Gentiles.

I want men everywhere to lift up holy hands in prayer, without anger or disputing. (2:1-8)

a. God's Word exhorts us to put prayer first.

If you were to disciple another believer, what would be at the top of your agenda for him or her? What would you challenge that person to do first? In this letter to Timothy, his "son" in the faith, Paul urges him to *pray*.

Paul says, "I urge, . . . first of all, that requests, prayers, intercession and thanksgiving be made for everyone." Of all the spiritual disciplines—Bible study, witnessing, stewardship of time and resources, hospitality, just to name a few—Paul singled out prayer as of first importance.

Someone asked Billy Graham the secret of his remarkable success in evangelism. Without hesitation, Graham responded that there were three secrets: prayer, prayer, prayer! Long before one of his crusades begins, Graham mobilizes thousands of people to pray. During a crusade meeting, while Graham is preaching, a host of people in an adjoining area are on their knees praying for the salvation of sinners listening to the evangelist.

Prayer brings God into the picture. It acknowledges the need for His Spirit's conviction. It calls upon Him to move sinners to repentance, to faith and to humble acceptance of Christ's saving grace.

Bill and Louise and two children visited a church in Ohio. The pastor and some of the lay people, looking at the visitor cards afterwards, noticed that the two adults had different family names.

"What's going on here?" the secretary asked. The pastor was himself unsure.

In the married couples' Sunday school class that they attended, someone asked them how long they had been married, and they replied, "Not yet!" Later the teacher asked the pastor what to do.

The pastor suggested that they pray about the matter and let the Lord work everything out appropriately. Those who were aware of the situation prayed earnestly. Two weeks later in the communion service, God brought deep conviction to both Bill and Louise.

Neither Bill nor Louise was in church the following week. But before long the pastor received a letter from Louise. In it she said she

had received Christ as her Savior while attending the church, and that in the communion service God made her realize she no longer could
live with someone else's husband. So she had
returned to her home state to live a new life
and to witness to her unsaved relatives.

Bill became reconciled with his estranged
wife. The family, including the two children,
have been reunited in a healed and happy
relationship and have become involved in a
Bible-believing church. Prayer certainly
changed both Bill and Louise's lives.

b. Prayer brings victory in battle.

> Timothy, my son, I give you this in-
> struction in keeping with the
> prophecies once made about you, so
> that by following them you may fight
> the good fight. (1:18)

The little word *then* (1 Timothy 2:1) is a
"hinge" word pointing back to the preceding
paragraph. Paul urges prayer because of something he has just mentioned. That something
was Paul's challenge to Timothy to "fight the
good fight." Timothy was in a battle. And so
are all committed followers of Christ, especially when they are praying for lost people!

Satan will not let one person put his or her
trust in Christ without a fight. He is irrevocably
opposed to God's interests. For that reason
Paul exhorted the Ephesian Christians to "put

on the full armor of God" (Ephesians 6:11). He continues, "Our struggle is not against flesh and blood, but against the rulers, . . . the authorities, . . . the powers of this dark world and against the spiritual forces of evil in the heavenly realms" (6:12). In light of such a battle, Paul exhorted the Christians in Ephesus to pray faithfully and fervently (6:18). He asked them as well to pray for him, that his communication of the gospel might be clear and courageous (6:19).

When I was a teenager my older brother had drifted away from God into a life of rebellion and deliberate sin. Realizing that Satan wanted to keep him from turning to Christ, Mother wrestled in prayer day and night for many years. During the mighty 1950 revival at Wheaton College, at 12 o'clock midnight, the Holy Spirit brought him under deep conviction and he surrendered his will and life to Christ. Prayer brought victory in battle and God used him for many years as a missionary and a pastor.

c. Prayer expresses faith in God.

> Fight the good fight, holding on to faith and a good conscience. Some have rejected these and so have shipwrecked their faith. (1:18b-19)

Twice here Paul refers to faith. Prayer on the lips expresses faith in the heart. My father taught me early in life that just the simple act of prayer was an expression of faith. By praying he was going to God in faith. For a missionary in Vietnam to raise a family of nine was a large step of faith!

Many times one of us would contract some kind of illness, and Dad, pointing to James chapter five, would go get his little oil bottle, gather the family around or call for some Vietnamese pastors and elders. Then he and they would pray very simply. When God healed us, people would marvel at Dad's faith. He explained to them that he didn't have any great faith; he just obeyed the Word of God to anoint the sick in the name of the Lord, and the rest was up to his miracle-working God!

2. The *pattern* of prayer

> I urge, then, first of all, that requests, prayers, intercession and thanksgiving be made for everyone. (2:1)

Paul considered prayer to be such an urgent matter that he used four different words to describe it. In so doing he gave us a pattern for praying. Each one of the words expresses a different and important facet of prayer.

a. Requests: Pray fervently.

James cites Elijah as an Old Testament example of a person who prayed fervently. "Elijah," James says, "was a man just like us.

He prayed earnestly that it would not rain, and it did not rain on the land for three and a half years. Again he prayed, and the heavens gave rain, and the earth produced its crops" (James 5:17-18).

Some people feel that to pray repeatedly and earnestly for something is an indication of weak faith. In his devotional classic, *Renewed Day by Day*, A.W. Tozer comments on such an attitude:

> I have met Christians who insist that it is wrong to pray for the same thing twice, the reason being that if we truly believe when we pray, we have the answer the first time; any second prayer betrays the unbelief of the first.
>
> There are three things wrong with this teaching. One is that it ignores a large body of Scripture; the second is that it rarely works in practice, even for the saintliest soul; and the third is that, if persisted in, it robs the praying man of two of his mightiest weapons in his warfare with the flesh and the devil: intercession and petition.
>
> For let it be said without qualification that the effective intercessor is never a one-prayer man, neither does the successful petitioner win his mighty resources in his first attempt!*

Renewed Day By Day (Vol. 1) by A.W. Tozer (Camp Hill, PA: Christian Publications, 1980). Entry for December 13.

For 10 years I prayed for my neighbors, Bill and Phyllis, along with several other neighbors. Then one day to my great delight they visited our church! They joined Donna's and my Sunday school class and our small group. Then Bill enrolled in our EE training and became a deacon in charge of greeting visitors. God has done a wonderful work in their lives. As I entreated God fervently each morning, He answered in His perfect time and way!

b. Prayers: Pray specifically.

Another "hang-up" that some people have with praying is the practice of petitioning God specifically. They over-simplify the situation, saying, "God knows everything and understands what's best anyhow, so why ask specifically? Just voice a general request and let Him work out the details. Write a blank check and let Him write in the amount."

But such general praying doesn't fit the biblical models. Jesus taught His disciples to pray "Give us today our daily bread," and God provided them bread. The early church prayed for Peter's deliverance from prison and prison doors opened! James says, "You do not have, because you do not ask God" (James 4:2).

For over 10 years at Christ Community Church a group of men has met early Saturday morning to pray specifically regarding our church's outreach. Among other things we prayed specifically for the planting of daughter churches in neighboring towns around Omaha. At first we prayed by name for the towns of Bellevue, Red Oak and Council Bluffs. One morning a man asked, "Why do we have to pray for places by name?" I responded that I believed God taught us to pray that way.

Amazingly, in April, 1984, God answered our prayers for all three places—all in the same month! I was able to launch a Bible study in Council Bluffs, Iowa, with 10 couples. Today there is a thriving church of approximately 200 believers in a lovely facility on 10 acres of land.

A former missionary from Vietnam started a Bible study in Bellevue, Nebraska, with a nucleus of our members who live in that area. Today that growing, healthy congregation is in a new church building of its own.

One Sunday morning two couples from Red Oak, Iowa, the third town for which we were praying, visited our worship service. They told an usher they wanted to meet me.

"A few weeks ago we visited our children at college in Orange City, Iowa," they explained. "While there on Sunday we attended an Alliance church. The church was having a missions conference. We had never been to one before and asked how we could have an Alliance church in our town. They told us that you were in charge of church planting in Omaha and could help us." Amazing! We started with those two couples and their families. Today there is a strong church in

Orange City, Iowa—perhaps the largest, most alive church in that town. The congregation has a dynamic pastor, a beautiful new facility and a missions conference which is just as exciting as the one in Orange City!

We prayed specifically for those three towns and God answered specifically and even beyond our wildest dreams! I should add that we went on to pray specifically for Wahoo, Missouri Valley, Plattsmouth and also for the Vietnamese, Hispanics, Hmong and African Americans in Omaha. Today, to the glory of God, He has answered these specific petitions, too. The churches are in various stages of development, but each has a pastor and is moving forward.

But perhaps you are asking what praying for new churches has to do with friendship evangelism. *New churches are centers for launching friendship evangelism in new communities.* These churches are growing because they are reaching out to unsaved people. That is the healthiest kind of church growth!

c. Intercession: Pray on behalf of others.

It's interesting that a little later in his first letter to Timothy, Paul describes Christ as the Mediator between God and humankind. He is the One "who gave himself as a ransom for all men" (2:6).

In a sense, you and I are also called to be mediators. We are to stand in prayer between

God and our FRANs, interceding for those who are yet lost.

If you have children and they are not following Christ, you have an urgent call to intercede for them, praying for their salvation. For some years Donna and I interceded for our son, Jeff. To me he seemed skeptical and indifferent about spiritual matters. The older he grew, the more callous he appeared to be. To make matters worse, eight months of the year Jeff was away from home at boarding school in Malaysia—far from where Donna and I were living and ministering in Vietnam. Letters just didn't communicate adequately. And during his vacation months at home, he evidenced no spiritual interest.

But of one thing Donna and I were certain. The great distance from Vietnam to Malaysia did not limit God from answering prayer! Nothing could keep God's Spirit from penetrating deep into Jeff's soul and conscience. So Donna and I prayed fervently for God to do what we couldn't.

One day we received a letter from Jeff. He said that while he was sitting by himself out in a field, he had done some serious thinking: "God," he had prayed, "I've been pretty stupid! You have been so good to me, but I haven't responded with faith in Christ." Right there and then Jeff yielded his life to Christ. And today he is serving God as a "tentmaking" missionary back in the land of his birth—Vietnam!

d. Thanksgiving: Pray expectantly.

Paul must have expected Timothy's prayers to be answered because he urged him to give thanks. When you pray, do you really expect God to answer or do you just go through motions, hoping that He might answer?

When we prayed for all those places where we thought a church was needed, we prayed expecting God to begin a new congregation in each one. It wasn't a question of whether but of when. When we are certain that something is God's will, He puts faith in our hearts—faith to believe Him for what we ask. Then we pray fervently and ceaselessly until He grants our request!

Fred, a heating and air-conditioning contractor, decided he had not impacted his business associates for Christ as totally as he should. After much prayer, he invited a number of them to his home for an evening Bible discussion. He sent an invitation by mail and followed it up with a personal telephone call. Fred invited a friend of his, Vern, to lead the discussion.

Over the course of 11 years, more than 3,000 different men attended those Bible discussions. Many of them Fred and Vern introduced to Jesus Christ and they later became members of Fred and Vern's church.

Did success like that just happen? Hardly. The two men prayed fervently, unceasingly. They gave thanks as they prayed. They prayed in faith until Satan and his evil emissaries had no power to stand against the gospel.

3. The *people* for whom you should pray

> I urge, then, first of all, that requests, prayers, intercession and thanksgiving be made for everyone—for kings and all those in authority, that we may live peaceful and quiet lives in all godliness and holiness. This is good, and pleases God our Savior, who wants all men to be saved and to come to a knowledge of the truth. For there is one God and one mediator between God and men, the man Christ Jesus, who gave himself as a ransom for all men—the testimony given in its proper time. And for this purpose I was appointed a herald and an apostle—I am telling the truth, I am not lying—and a teacher of the true faith to the Gentiles. (2:1-7)

Notice that Paul exhorted Timothy to pray, not for buildings, books, organizations, programs but for *people!* People are what life and ministry are all about! Your home, your car, your business, the money you have accumulated—none of it can you take with you to heaven. *People* are all that you can take. Husband, wife, children, grandchildren, friends, relatives, associates, neighbors—they are the priceless coinage of life. If you are living with eternity's values in view, you will be focused on people. God has put you on planet earth and made you one of His own so you can witness to and win people!

Paul suggests that Timothy pray for two classes of people: One, kings and all who are in authority and, two, all men.

a. Pray for your leaders.

Both in the Old and New Testaments, God's people have through prayer influenced governments and armies. Through prayer Isaiah saw the armies of Sennacherib turned back defeated (Isaiah 37). The church at Jerusalem prayed, and Peter was released from prison—and Herod was destroyed by worms (Acts 12).

Do you know that you can impact those who rule in your land? Do you know that you can influence the direction your nation is heading? Do you know that you literally can advance the cause of the gospel worldwide?

In the late 19th century a pastor, Albert Benjamin Simpson, was seen in his study embracing a globe of the world, placing his finger on nation after nation still without the gospel of Jesus Christ. He prayed that God would open those nations to the good news of His Son. As he prayed, tears coursed down his face and onto the world globe.

Not so many years later, missionaries from Simpson's own church were entering many of those lands for which he prayed. My missionary parents helped pioneer Vietnam, Ellison and Hammond entered Cambodia, Voth moved into Laos, Fisk evangelized the aborigines of Borneo. Roseberry went to West Africa, Barnes to Argentina—and the list goes on and on.

When government and military leaders threatened the advance of Christ's kingdom, Christians prayed and God has overthrown or turned back opposing forces.

Does this have any bearing on friendship evangelism? Indeed it does! First, God commands us to pray for our national leaders and all who have authority over us. Second, should we not be praying for God to open doors to nations without Christ so that we can make known His salvation to the ends of the earth? Third, on our shrinking globe, friendships more and more cross national and international boundaries.

A few years ago at Christ Community Church, we initiated after much prayer a series of October evangelistic events that we called Fall Spectaculars. The objective was to take the gospel out into the Omaha community with guest speakers like Josh McDowell, astronaut Jim Irwin and football star Jeff Seimon.

Each year for six years we brought our speakers to, among other places, the Air Force Strategic Air Command base. About 100 top Air Force officers gathered for an evangelistic breakfast each year. What a privilege it was to uncompromisingly present the gospel to some of the highest ranking officers in our land. A number of them received Christ into their lives, including one four-star general. God truly answered our prayers!

b. Pray for the salvation of your FRANs.

Paul exhorted Timothy to pray for all men that they might understand the truth and be saved. Paul reminds Timothy of God's saving plan through His Son, the infinite God-Man, the Mediator between God and humankind, the One who laid down His life as a ransom for our sins.

It is possible in a general way to pray for all people, but impossible for any one person to pray specifically for all people. But there are specific people in your network of relationships for whom you can and should pray. In fact, there's nothing any better that you can do for your FRANs than to pray for them.

"But," you ask, "how in practical terms do I pray for my FRANs?" In EE we suggest that you draw up a list of at least 10 of them, developing a profile for each. Then we suggest that you pray specifically, fervently, regularly and expectantly for them. Next we suggest that you begin to look for ways to express the love of Christ to them in practical, meaningful ways, being especially aware of their moments of need and looking for opportunities to share the gospel with them. EE also offers a little booklet, "Partners in Praying," that will help you pray for your FRANs and apply the above steps to bring them to Christ.

Friends: For seven years Kim prayed fervently for her best friend's 29-nine-year-old unsaved husband. Finally, one evening she brought her youth EE team to visit him and share the gospel with him. As her 14-year-old trainee shared the gospel with this man, Kim was amazed to see God move him to receive Christ as his personal Savior.

Relatives: Mrs. Lourdes prayed for many years for three of her family members. In fact, every Sunday she put a note in the offering plate asking her pastor and his staff to pray for them. One happy day an elder from our church, Steve, had the joy of leading all three of her relatives to Christ.

Associates: Remember Fred and his business associates? One night the Bible discussion group was so large that they had to move it from Fred's house to the home of a wealthy construction company owner. That evening 165 men gathered. Fourteen of them were converted.

Neighbors: Mark heard that his neighbor across the street had received a diagnosis of cancer. He prayed for her and at the appropriate time visited her. She listened attentively as he shared the gospel, but she was not then ready to commit her life to Christ. As her cancer spread, she had to be hospitalized. Not long before she died, she called a Christian friend and asked her to help her trust Christ as Savior. Then she asked this friend to thank her neighbor, Mark, for his prayers and for bringing her the good news of Christ.

Strangers: Sometimes God opens a door of opportunity for you into the life of a total stranger. One Sunday morning in Hong Kong, just a half hour before our worship service was to begin, I received a phone call from a stranger. She said she and her husband had just arrived from Singapore.

"What do you think of Christian Science?" she asked me over the phone. I felt uncomfortable answering such a question over the phone, especially coming from someone I had never met. So I asked her to explain why she asked.

"My husband has a large cancerous growth located behind his right ear. That's why we've come to Hong Kong. I'm told that Christian Science churches believe in healing," she responded.

"Our church believes in diving healing. Why don't you visit us this morning?" I suggested, giving her the address and the time of our service.

The couple came immediately and greeted me after the worship hour. I invited them to our visitor reception and introduced them to a number of people from our church. As the group was breaking up, I said to the couple, "I would like to visit you in your home and pray there. May I bring along a couple of friends?"

They agreed, and we set a time.

One member of my visitation team was a church elder. The other was a woman I was training in EE. At the appointed time the three of us reached the place where the Singapore couple was staying. After we had all become better acquainted, I asked the couple the two EE diagnostic questions to determine where they stood with God. The wife turned out to be a genuine believer. Although her husband went to church occasionally, he was uncertain about his faith. I explained that before we could pray for his healing, we needed to be sure he was on "praying ground." We shared the gospel and he invited Christ into his life.

After that, I read from James 5 where he directs the sick to call for the elders of the church, who will anoint and pray for the sick person. I reminded my new friend that he had confessed his sins, as James suggests. In obedience to the Scriptures, I anointed the man with oil. We prayed very simply in faith for God to heal him. And then my team and I went home rejoicing in the man's salvation and trusting God for his healing.

The couple came regularly to our worship services and joined a home Bible study. They had a new joy that infected our whole congregation. About six weeks later, the wife called to inform us that they were moving back to Singapore. She wanted to know if Donna and I could join them for a farewell luncheon.

When we arrived at the restaurant, the wife pointed behind her husband's ear.

"Look," she exclaimed, "it's just like baby skin. The doctor can't understand it and has informed my husband that the cancer is gone! Healed!"

Of course, Donna and I rejoiced with them in the husband's healing, but even more in the couple's being united in Christ as an answer to prayer!

4. The *places* where you should pray

> I want men everywhere to lift up holy hands in prayer, without anger or disputing. (2:8)

Paul told Timothy he wanted men to pray in every place, lifting holy hands heavenward. This suggests two things about God: First, God can be at work wherever you are. Second, God can be glorified wherever you are.

a. Through prayer God will be at work wherever you are.

Paul wants believers to pray everywhere. Prayer is not limited to the sanctuary or the prayer closet. Anywhere and everywhere you can pray: while driving on the highway, at the work place, in the office, at the kitchen sink, on the ball field or in the classroom.

A new type of praying is sweeping through many parts of our land. It's called "prayer walking" and is as simple as an individual going for a walk around the block while he or she prays. It can also be as complex as a city-wide campaign where pastors get out maps, divide up the neighborhoods between churches and systematically walk every street in the course of a year.

Cynthia, mother of three, started prayer walking four years ago. "When my husband and I first moved in," she writes, "we began to walk through the streets every day, praying for every one of the 28 homes in our neighbor-hood. We prayed for every family, eventually learning their names and knowing some of their needs. Within six months we started a Bible study in our home with the folks we had been praying for. It wasn't long before we saw four of our neighbors commit their lives to the Lord."*

If you are serious about wanting to see people in your network of relationships come to know Christ, why not surround them with prayer wherever they are? When you are at work, pray silently for your boss and fellow employees. When you are walking or driving in your neighborhood, pray for those in the homes around you. When you are at your sports club, pray for those you regularly meet there. And as you pray, ask God to give you an

Prayer Walking by Steve Hawthorne and Graham Kendrick (Orlando, FL: Creation House, 1993). p. 10.

opening to share Christ with them or to invite them to an evangelistic event at your church.

b. Through prayer God is glorified wherever you are.

It is significant that Paul commands men to raise holy hands heavenward. Hands extended heavenward acknowledge God and give Him glory for what He has done or is about to do.

I have already told you about Lisa, the Spanish-speaking New Yorker who brought her English-speaking husband, Raymond, to church to hear me preach and afterwards preempted some of my limited dinner hour to help Raymond to "be saved."

It was like picking ripe fruit. Lisa evidently had prayed for Raymond so long and so fervently that God had softened his heart. After Raymond had invited Christ into his life, I looked over at Lisa. Tears were running down her cheeks. When Raymond saw how much his coming to Christ meant to his wife, a big smile broke across his face.

Lisa had prayed for her husband's salvation for a long time. How happy she was! We didn't raise our hands heavenward, but maybe we should have, because God certainly was glorified through His answer to prayer!

How does God want to use you to pray people to Christ? May He move you today to get started in this wonderful ministry.

Discussion Questions

1. Why do you think Paul gave prayer such a high priority in his life? Why did he recommend it to Timothy as the first priority?

2. What exactly is the pattern Paul gave Timothy and gives us?

3. What would you say to a person who says it is sufficient to pray once for something and that to pray more than that evidences a lack of faith?

4. According to Paul, who should we pray for regularly? For what should we pray in regard to them?

5. Where should we pray? Explain.

Chapter Twelve

Maximizing Divine Appointments

John 4:4-42

AT SOME TIME OR another you probably met a person in a manner that appeared to be accidental, but which, in fact, God arranged. It happened to me as I was flying back to Omaha from the EE clinic at Walden, New York, mentioned in the previous chapter. A few days later I was scheduled to teach a clinic in Omaha.

"Lord," I prayed, "I've been *talking* a lot about witnessing. Now, I ask You, please give me an opportunity to *do* some witnessing!"

As I settled into my Ozark Airline aisle seat, I introduced myself to the young woman sitting by the window. Her name was Tammy. She was employed by a large real estate company in San Antonio, Texas. Tammy and I exchanged a few pleasantries about the weather and the flight. When Tammy buried her face in a magazine, I also reached for a magazine. And I prayed, "Lord, if You want me to talk to her about eternal matters, You're going to have to cause her to put that magazine away."

Half an hour later a tantalizing fragrance floated down the aisle and the flight attendants began serving dinner. The meal featured steak, which prompted a comment from Tammy.

"Flying to New York they didn't serve us steak," she reported. "Isn't this a bit unusual?"

"Well, yes," I replied. "I don't get steak very often on my flights either."

"You sound like you do a lot of flying," Tammy continued. "What do you do?"

"Oh, I'm a pastor," I explained. "I hold clinics for pastors and laypeople in various places across America."

"I didn't know pastors flew that much! I used to be involved in church myself," Tammy added, "until my divorce a few months ago. Now I've kind of got away from religion and church."

Tammy's last comment led very naturally into my talking about the purpose of the church as well as my church and my personal testimony. Before the plane touched down in Louisville, Tammy had given her heart to Christ. I asked her for her address so I could refer her to a good church in San Antonio.

As we were landing, Tammy remarked, "You know what, Tom? I think God put you on this plane just for me!"

"I call it a 'divine appointment'!" I replied.

To maximize God-given opportunities for witness, you need to be alert and prepared.

Jesus experienced a similar divine appointment when the Samaritan woman in Sychar came to Jacob's well for water. Before Jesus left her, He had given her living water—the gift of eternal life (John 4:4-42). As I look more closely at the sequence of events, I discover five reasons why every Christian, in such chance meetings with other people, needs to be alert and equipped.

1. They're *strangers*

[Jesus] had to go through Samaria. So he came to a town in Samaria called Sychar, near the plot of ground Jacob had given to his son Joseph. Jacob's well was there, and Jesus, tired as he was from the journey, sat down by the well. It was about the sixth hour.

When a Samaritan woman came to draw water, Jesus said to her, "Will you give me a drink?" (His disciples had gone into the town to buy food.)

The Samaritan woman said to him, "You are a Jew and I am a Samaritan woman. How can you ask me for a drink?" (For Jews do not associate with Samaritans.) (John 4:4-9)

Jesus and His disciples, on their way from Judea to Galilee, chose the more direct route through Samaria. They stopped at Jacob's well on the outskirts of Sychar, and the disciples went into town to buy some food. Jesus remained at the well and so He was there when the village woman came with an empty pitcher to draw water.

It was evidently the first contact Jesus had had with the Samaritan woman, although in His omniscience He knew her. To the Samaritan woman Jesus was a Stranger. But the fact that the two had not previously met didn't prevent Jesus from reaching out to the woman with the gospel of salvation.

Until this chapter, I have been urging you to reach those with whom you already have a relationship: friends, relatives, associates and neighbors. I have emphasized over and over that these "FRANs" are the most responsive people you can evangelize. But, of course, that doesn't mean you should avoid witnessing to people you've never met before. Jesus witnessed to the woman at the well. I shared Christ with Tammy. Both women were total strangers to the person witnessing to them, yet God had prepared their hearts. And when given the chance, they both came to the Savior.

a. You may differ in culture and gender.

The Samaritan woman expressed surprise that Jesus would even speak to her. Customarily, Jews and Samaritans did not converse. They had no cross-cultural associations.

Moreover, there was the gender problem. No doubt the woman was also surprised that Jesus, a Man, would deign even to make a request of her, a woman with whom He was unacquainted. Perhaps, like Tammy, she would have buried her face in a magazine had there been magazines at hand in that day.

Ofttimes people of one culture are caught off guard when someone of another culture seeks to establish rapport. They are so accustomed to racial prejudice that the smallest kindness opens their hearts to the gospel.

Bill, an elderly believer at Christ Community Church in Omaha, has an unusual love for people of other cultures. When he encounters them at a mall or in a supermarket, he introduces himself to them. He invites them to his home for breakfast. He develops a relationship with them and often brings them to church. Many of them have come to Christ as a result of Bill's loving concern for them.

Others through our ministry called FOCUS (Friendship to Overseas College and University Students) have entertained international students in their homes for Christmas, Thanksgiving and Easter. Or they've organized a potluck dinner, a hay ride or a birthday party for such students. This has led to the formation of a Sunday school class just for international students. One such student from China has gone through our New Beginnings class for new believers and new members!

North America is a melting pot for people of many cultures. If you will be alert, you can be a "missionary" to some of these without leaving your hometown! Many of them are eager for your loving witness. And by exercising discretion, as Jesus did at the well and as I did on the flight to Louisville, you can even witness to those of the other gender.

b. You may find it inconvenient.

Jesus was tired (4:6). He was thirsty (4:7). He was hungry (4:8). Yet those excuses did not prevent Him from reaching out to a needy woman.

After teaching day and night for a week in Walden, New York, I was exhausted. I could have pushed my seat back and taken a long rest. Instead, I sought opportunity to share the gospel with Tammy. As a result, she gave her heart to Jesus Christ.

On another occasion, I had just finished preaching to an Hispanic congregation in downtown Manhattan. My wife, Donna, and I were standing with Pastor Roberto and one of my team members, Wayne, on the sidewalk in front of the church waiting to cross the street.

Pastor Roberto had invited us to have Sunday dinner with him at a nearby Greek restaurant. I was tired and hungry. And in just an hour I would be participating in the Vietnamese worship service held also in the Hispanic church.

Right at that moment a member of the Hispanic congregation approached me with her Caucasian husband.

"Pastor, I'm Lisa and this is my husband, Raymond. He doesn't speak Spanish, so he doesn't usually attend church with me. Could you pray for him?"

It was a rather indefinite request. "In what way can I pray for him?" I asked.

"To be saved, Pastor," Lisa responded.

I asked Wayne if he would stay and help the couple.

"Tom, I think we need to go with the pastor to the restaurant," Wayne countered. He was being careful that we not offend our host. And that was good.

At that very instant a struggle went on in my mind. It's amazing how in a few split seconds all kinds of thoughts can race through your brain! I saw Jesus by the well at Sychar talking to the Samaritan woman. I heard the disciples saying to Him, "Eat something." I recalled Jesus' insistence that He had a more important agenda than physical food. But I also struggled with hunger pangs and weariness.

"Well, maybe we should go back into the pastor's study," I heard myself saying to Lisa.

On the way up the steps I asked Raymond about his family and work. I asked him how long he had lived in New York. I normally try to take more time to build a relationship, but our time together was short. He needed to take Lisa home for dinner and I had another service coming up.

Evidently Lisa had had a good testimony before her husband, because Raymond was very open and responsive. She had reflected Christ in her home and had planted good seed in his heart. It was my task to share the gospel clearly, simply and then give the man the opportunity to receive Christ. When we were through praying, I looked over at Lisa. Tears were running down her cheeks. I looked at Raymond. He was evidently touched by her joy and emotion, because a big bright smile swept across his face.

At that point, my friend Wayne returned from a hastily eaten dinner. Welcoming Raymond into God's family, I turned over the immediate follow-up to Wayne and excused myself to join Pastor Roberto and my wife, Donna, at the Greek restaurant.

Rather often God's divine appointments come disguised in very inconvenient circumstances. Recently, a woman came to Christ stating that what really attracted her to the Savior was the concern of a young man who pulled his car off the highway and gave her a ride when her own car broke down on the interstate. Her decision was clinched when a group of compassionate people from the same church at great inconvenience to themselves helped her find a place to live when she suddenly became homeless.

c. You must cultivate their friendship.

John's description of how Jesus built a friendship with the Samaritan woman covers 12 of the 38 verses devoted to Jesus' sojourn at Sychar. Aware that His visit with the woman would be necessarily brief, Jesus nevertheless took time to become acquainted and to establish rapport. Only after that did He present the gospel to her.

Often it takes more than one encounter to bring a person from total ignorance of the gospel to a genuine commitment to Christ. But when God prepares a person and gives you a divine appointment similar to Jesus' with the Samaritan woman, you can establish a friendship and lead the person to faith in Christ in one encounter! But, like Jesus, you need to take time to establish a friendship.

One day Jack shared with me his joy in leading to Christ one of his customers, a pharmacist in Weber, Nebraska. Weber is a Czech town, predominantly Roman Catholic. The pharmacist was Czechoslovakian, so Jack took plenty of time to find out about that culture and other factors in his friend's background. Before the two parted from lunch, they bowed in prayer and the Czech pharmacist trusted Christ as his personal Savior.

"Jack," I asked, "how are you able to reach so many of your customers, friends, employees and even total strangers for Christ?"

"Well, Pastor," he answered, "first I try to be very, very friendly. I try with God's help to come across very warm and loving. My goal is to be totally nonthreatening with no selfish motives or agenda. I listen carefully, and when dealing with businessmen I follow good business principles. I usually try to share my personal testimony before I move into the gospel. Also, when fellow Christians know I'm equipped to share the gospel, they often bring their friends to me and ask me to win them to Christ. The secret is to be equipped and to be warm and friendly!"

I've observed Jack in action. I understand why people are totally disarmed by his loving, gracious and forthright approach. I can see why they are so responsive to his invitation to trust Christ.

2. They're *searching*

The Samaritan woman had come to Jacob's well for water—water that would never totally satisfy. The water that she was drawing from the well was a symbol of everything else she was drawing upon to try to satisfy her heart's craving. Evidently she had presumed that illicit sexual relationships would bring her some kind of fulfillment. According to Jesus, she had had five husbands, and the man with whom she was living wasn't her husband. The Samaritan woman is an incredibly accurate picture of the searching people all around you and me.

a. They have a deep void in their lives.

You might call it a "God-shaped vacuum": emptiness, dissatisfaction, frustration, unmet goals, unfulfilled cravings. They're like the frustrated, frantically determined dachshund that A.W. Tozer graphically described "chasing breathlessly after its tail—a tail, incidentally, which is not there because it has previously been removed."

b. They're exploring various alternatives.

Like the Samaritan woman with her variety of men, sinners the world around search for meaning and fulfillment in possessions, popularity, pleasure, power, people. But like Solomon, who tried it all, they usually conclude that all is vanity. The best the world can offer just doesn't last. It doesn't give what human beings really want. That's because . . .

c. They want what only God can give.

The God-shaped vacuum can only be filled by God—God in the Person of Jesus Christ! Thousands, millions have testified that, like Tammy on the Ozark Airline flight, their lifelong search never ended until, at last, they found the Savior. And guess what?

d. You can end their lifelong search!

By lovingly, tactfully introducing them to the Savior, you can bring their search to a satisfying, joyous conclusion. Of course in any witnessing situation, you won't want to jump right in and, without any lead-in, ask the person, "Are you saved?" But like Jesus at the well, after you have built a bridge of friendship, after you have gradually moved from the person's interests in secular things to spiritual matters, you can share a personal testimony and give a brief, clear presentation of the gospel.

The best way to prepare for this is to take some training in personal evangelism, such as Evangelism Explosion. If you haven't had the opportunity, you might want to walk them through a gospel tract such as "Do You Know for Sure?" published by Evangelism Explosion or "Have You Heard of the Four Spiritual Laws?" issued by Campus Crusade.

I was preaching in Mechanicsburg, Pennsylvania, and at the end of my Sunday morning message I gave an invitation. As people made their way to the front, the pastor told me that he and the elders would handle the counseling at the altar. He asked me to greet worshipers at the door as they left the sanctuary. As the number of people began to dwindle, two young men, Joe and Bryan, came by to shake my hand. As Joe shook my hand, he spotted the two-question-mark pin on the lapel of my suit.

"What are the question marks about?" he asked.

"Oh, those represent two of the most important questions anyone ever asked me," I answered. Joe wanted to know what they were.

"Every presidential candidate at the last election was asked those two questions," I added. By then, Joe's curiosity was really piqued.

"But what are the questions?" he demanded again.

"I never share these questions unless a person assures me that he will answer them." I said. Both Joe and Bryan agreed to answer the two questions.

I suspected that Bryan was from the church and that Joe was his guest, so I asked Joe the questions first. Joe told me he hoped he'd go to heaven, because he wasn't on drugs and lived a clean life. Bryan knew he was heaven bound. He was trusting Christ alone for eternal life.

I told Joe I had some wonderful news to share with him and asked if he was in a hurry. Both fellows said they had time, so I invited them into the pastor's study. About a half hour later Joe gave his heart to Christ. The pastor gave him a Bible and I gave him a signed spiritual birth certificate.

As Joe and Bryan left, Bryan said, "Thank you, Pastor, for helping Joe trust Christ. I've been praying for him for a year. I brought him to church today hoping he'd find Christ as his Savior."

Joe thanked me as well. "And thank you, too," he added, "for wearing that pin on your lapel to catch my attention!" More recently the church pastor told me that Joe had married a fine Christian girl and is going on with Christ. Joe's search for satisfaction ended when he found Christ that joyful Sunday morning.

3. They're *sinning*

Sin is no longer the pejorative word it once was—except in God's ears. The Holy Spirit came to "convict the world of guilt in regard to sin" (John 16:8). Adulterous David confessed to God, "Against you, you only, have I sinned and done what is evil in your sight, so that you are proved right when you speak and justified when you judge" (Psalm 51:4).

a. They're trying to satisfy a God-given appetite in an illegitimate way.

That's what sin is. It's the corrupting of something wholesome and good by seeking to enjoy it in an unlawful manner. Eating is a legitimate and wonderful God-given function. But gluttony is a sin. Sex between a husband and wife is a beautiful thing. But adultery is sin. Fornication is sin.

b. They'll never find lasting satisfaction in sin.

After whatever immediate pleasurable sensation wears off the forbidden act, ugly realization sets in: Sin, like crime, doesn't pay. Quite the opposite, it brings pain, anguish, shame, scars, judgment and death. The Samaritan woman surely knew this and was ready for a change. But both she and . . .

c. They must deal honestly and thoroughly with sin.

Before people can find forgiveness, cleansing, hope and salvation, they must realize what sin is. They must comprehend its awful degrading influence. They must understand its painful results in the present and the dreadful judgment it will receive in the future.

Jesus did not evade the subject of sin. He knew that unless the Samaritan woman faced up to her sin, she could never find what she was really searching for. And in dealing with her sin Jesus found, and . . .

d. You will find sin a very sensitive subject to talk about.

Notice how very gently Jesus approached the subject. He took care not to alienate the woman:

"He told her, 'Go, call your husband and come back' " (4:16).

"I have no husband" (4:17). From her answer it was evident that she realized her culpability. I'd like to suggest to you a four-step gradual, nonjudgmental approach to helping people admit that they are sinners.

First, state that all people are sinners. There is Bible backing for your assertion in Romans 3:23.

Second, define sin as the transgression of God's law in thought, word or deed.

Third, mention that even some of the most honored and respected people—for example, David and Paul—labeled themselves sinners.

Fourth, ask the person you are counseling if he or she will admit to ever having sinned. Notice that Jesus solicited an admission from the Samaritan that she had sinned. That is the beginning of confession that leads to genuine repentance.

After the wall between East and West Germany came down, I was in Karlmarkstad, East Germany, preaching for four days to North Vietnamese who were working to pay off war debts. After each message, I invited those who wanted to trust Christ to come to a room on the second floor where I could counsel them without distractions.

After one of the services, two men and a woman came for counseling. I spent about half an hour with them clarifying the plan of salvation. Then they were ready to pray. As I led them in a prayer of repentance and faith, I noticed that one of them—the woman—wasn't praying. So I paused and asked what was wrong.

"Oh," she explained, "you said in your prayer that I'm a sinner. But I've never sinned, so I couldn't pray after you." I suddenly realized I hadn't defined sin in terms she could understand. So I read and explained each of the Ten Commandments. The woman admitted that she had broken all of them. With an understanding of sin, she was ready to pray and to receive the forgiveness and eternal life which Christ alone offers.

4. They're worth *saving*

When God created Adam, He made him special. He made him "in his own image" (Genesis 1:27). He "breathed into his nostrils the breath of life, and the man became a living being" (2:7).

God intended for humankind, in whose hearts God set eternity (see Ecclesiastes 3:11), to glorify Him on earth and enjoy Him forever.

Alas, the Bible is the sad record of how Adam and his progeny deliberately and consistently departed from God's ways. But the Bible is more: It is the record of God's enduring love for humankind and His provision through Jesus Christ, His Son, to save His human creation from their sins (see John 3:16). If God loved humankind enough to give His one and only Son to die that they might be saved, then people are worth saving.

a. They need to know who Jesus is.

At first, as I observed earlier, the Samaritan woman thought Jesus was just a Jew (4:9). Then she perceived that He was a prophet (4:19). Then she learned that He was the Messiah (4:25). Finally, she came to trust him as

Savior (4:42). Today, it's the same. If people would be saved . . .

b. They need to know Jesus came to save them.

Jesus told the Samaritan woman that salvation came from the Jewish people (4:22). He, Jesus, was a Jew. He had come to give her eternal life (4:14). So people today need to understand that they cannot save themselves. They need Jesus Christ Who came to provide for them eternal life. And . . .

c. They need to place their trust in Him.

Biblical, saving faith is, at first, difficult for people to comprehend. You must distinguish clearly between mental assent, temporal faith and saving trust. People need to know how to transfer their trust from their own efforts to save themselves to the finished work of Jesus Christ on the cross.

d. You can help them take this important step.

It's apparent that Jesus helped the woman at the well put her trust in Him. So convinced was she of His saving grace that she forgot her water pot at the well and ran off to the city to testify to her new life in Christ! She was so excited about what happened to her that she started sharing the good news of her Savior with others. When people come to Christ today . . .

5. They too can begin *sharing*

Good news is to be shared! It is important that new believers share their faith with friends, relatives, associates and neighbors. They demonstrate the reality of what has happened in their lives when they start sharing.

Anyone who has been genuinely converted, who has tasted and seen that the Lord is good, will want to share his or her discovery with others. It is an accurate statement that . . .

a. A "satisfied customer" is the gospel's best advertisement.

The person who buys a car he or she really likes will begin talking to friends about how good that car is. When someone discovers a dream vacation spot for an amazingly low price, he or she passes on the secret to his or her best friends. The scientist who discovers a reliable cure for a life-threatening illness wants the whole world to know about it. Likewise new believers, like the woman at the well, when truly converted and gloriously satisfied, can become some of the best evangelists anywhere!

Our church's short-term missionary team was in Freetown, Sierra Leone, Africa, training African pastors in an Evangelism Explosion clinic. Over the lunch hour we decided to walk through the center of town for some sightseeing.

As we walked past the main park, one of our

team members, Jim, suddenly spotted a young African walking toward us reading what looked like a gospel tract. Quickly Jim stopped, said goodbye to the rest of us and struck up a conversation with the young man.

Indeed, the African was reading a tract which someone else in town had given him. And, yes, he was very interested in the gospel. After an extended conversation with Jim, the young man, John, gave his heart to Christ. Jim told him where we were staying and urged him to come see him the next day for some more follow-up discipling.

When John appeared at the beginning of our lunch break the next day, he had his brother with him! John was so convinced that the gospel was the truth and what he needed that he persuaded his brother to meet Jim and to find Christ! John demonstrated that his faith was real when he started sharing it with others.

b. They can lead to many other seekers.

The Bible informs us, "Many of the Samaritans from that town believed in [Jesus] because of the woman's testimony, 'He told me everything I ever did.' " (4:39). No doubt the woman went back and brought many of her friends, relatives, associates and neighbors to Christ. Christ shared His gospel with a stranger. Then He used her to witness to her *oikos*. And this is the way the gospel spreads. This is the method by which the kingdom of Christ was extended in the first century. The quotation I shared in a previous chapter bears repeating: "Lead me to a new believer and I'll show you a whole nest of potentially responsive people." Therefore, I conclude that . . .

c. Reproduction is the secret of multiplication.

Jesus led one stranger to faith in Himself and sent her back to her friends, relatives, associates and neighbors. And many from her town also turned to Him. This was the secret of multiplication in the early church, and it will work the same today!

When I was pastoring an English-speaking congregation in Hong Kong, 1976 to 1979, I met a young man, Edmund, following one of our Sunday morning services. His father had died in an elevator accident in Manila. The body was flown back to Hong Kong for burial. Since some of the family members were believers, they visited our church. Edmund was their driver. I invited him to stay for refreshments on the church patio.

There he met a young woman, Judi. In the course of their conversation, the two discovered they had a common experience, for Judi's father had also died that year. Judi said she was comforted to know that her dad was in heaven. Edmund wasn't sure anyone could know that.

When Edmund mentioned that he was an optometrist, Judi expressed interest in buying some contact lenses from him. On that trip they talked some more, and Judi realized Edmund seemed open to the gospel. She asked if she might bring a couple of friends to his home for a visit.

At the first visit, Judi didn't feel they had gotten anywhere with Edmund, so she asked if she might return with two other friends. Still Edmund was not ready to commit himself to Christ. So Judi asked Edmund if he would be willing to go to the parsonage and visit with me and my team. That night Edmund trusted Christ as his Savior.

Edmund signed up for evangelism training and in a short time became an enthusiastic witness. A couple of years after I returned to the United States, he called me from California to say he was on his way to Fort Lauderdale, Florida, for training as an EE clinic teacher.

"Edmund," I asked, "how many people have you seen come to Christ since I left Hong Kong?"

"Twenty-six!" Edmund replied.

How exciting it has been since then to see Edmund not simply win people to Christ but also train scores of others who are winning people to Christ! Truly reproduction is the secret of multiplication.

Ask God to show you what you need to do to be ready for the divine appointments He sends your way. Then begin!

Discussion Questions

1. What do you understand a "divine appointment" to be? Have you ever encountered one? If so how did it turn out?

2. If friendship or relational evangelism is the most biblical and effective, do you believe it is appropriate to share the gospel with strangers? Why or why not?

3. What about sharing the gospel with a person of the other gender or another culture?

4. If such an "appointment" is inconvenient for you, how can it still be called "divine"?

5. Is it possible in one encounter to build a bridge of friendship strong enough to share the gospel effectively? Why do you say yes or no?

6. How can a person deal with the delicate subject of sin in a sensitive yet effective way?

7. Can a new believer—one who has just received Christ—be an effective witness? Explain.

Chapter Thirteen

Doing It Jesus' Way

John 21:1-22

FOLLOWING ONE OF Dwight L. Moody's crusades, a rather belligerent church member came up to the evangelist. "Mr. Moody," he said, "I don't like the way you evangelize!"

Showing no animosity, Moody responded calmly, "And how do *you* evangelize?"

"I haven't found a way yet," the man admitted.

Never at a loss for words, Moody replied, "Well, I guess I like the way I evangelize better than the way you don't!"

Obviously there is more than one way you can reach your non-Christian friends, relatives, associates and neighbors. Maybe you are trying to decide which way is best. Or perhaps you already have a good, workable method. You may be saying in your heart, "You can do it your way and I'll do it mine." Then again, perhaps you haven't come up with a "best" way to win your FRANs to Christ.

I hope you will not consider me too dogmatic when I assert that *true evangelistic success comes to those who evangelize Jesus' way.*

While Jesus was on earth, He gave His disciples a mandate to witness. But He also gave them several models of how to witness. One such model He gave to His disciples on the banks of the Sea of Galilee (also called the Sea of Tiberias) after His resurrection from the dead. It is Christ's last recorded lesson on evangelism; it may well have been His most important one.

Let's join Jesus' disciples and learn five important lessons about evangelism.

1. Fellowshiping

> Afterward Jesus appeared again to his disciples, by the Sea of Tiberias. It happened this way: Simon Peter, Thomas (called Didymus), Nathanael from Cana in Galilee, the sons of Zebedee, and two other disciples were together. "I'm going out to fish," Simon Peter told them, and they said, "We'll go with you." So they went out

and got into the boat, but that night
they caught nothing. (21:1-3)

The word *fellowship* in the New Testament
comes from a root word meaning to have in
common or to share. Hence Christian fellowship
is simply to share our common life in Christ.

Someone has defined fellowship as "two or
more fellows together in the same ship"! If that
is the case, then we have a classic example of
fellowship in this narrative, for John informs us
that seven of Jesus' disciples were together in
the boat.

The Scriptures teach about fellowship.
Churches large and small offer Christian fellowship. But when we examine the various
kinds of fellowship being offered today, we
must conclude that . . .

a. There is no sweeter fellowship than that which has a saving purpose.

Fellowship together while fishing can be fun.
Coffee fellowships are enjoyable. Bible study
fellowships are edifying. Prayer fellowships see
a lot accomplished for God's kingdom. But
there's just nothing so exhilarating as partner-
ing with someone to bring a person to Christ
Jesus. When you have a role in that, you are
doing something of lasting value, something
eternal! You are being instrumental in making
it possible for your friend to discover fellowship with God not only in this world, but

forever in heaven!

For many years Donna and I served in different types of ministry. I focused my vision, gifts and energy on evangelism, discipleship, church planting, preaching and administration while she was involved in children's and women's ministries, hospitality and, of course, homemaking.

While serving as missionary pastor of the English-speaking congregation in Hong Kong that I alluded to earlier, I stumbled onto Evangelism Explosion. It provided what I had been looking for to equip my flock for friendship evangelism. One of the first persons I trained was Donna, my wife. She was reticent to become involved, assuming that she had to have a so-called "gift of evangelism" in order to witness effectively. When I convinced her from the Word that every believer is to be a witness and that with a little training she could win people to Christ, she joined me in the ministry.

In addition to serving together in Hong Kong and Omaha, Nebraska, Donna and I have taken short-term missions teams all over the world. For 17 years she and I have enjoyed wonderful fellowship in winning people to Christ, in training other evangelists and in equipping fellow pastors and missionaries. Donna has trained pastors on practically every continent and they write thanking her for training them. Speaking of teams, . . .

b. Teamwork is essential to effective evangelism.

Fishermen who, like the first century disciples, fish for a living, who are serious about fishing, know the importance of teamwork. Every member has a function. When the net is full of fish, all grab hold and pull together. Once the catch is in, some take the fish to market, others wash and mend the nets, some care for maintenance of the boat. When those early disciples left their nets to fish for men, they knew well the importance of cooperative effort.

Some Christians excuse themselves from personal evangelism by saying, "I don't have the gift of evangelism." They need to meet Anne Kennedy, wife of EE founder D. James Kennedy. Anne admits, "I don't have the gift of evangelism—just the gift of obedience."

Anne Kennedy has been active in the evangelism equipping ministry of her church since its inception more than 30 years ago. When her husband is greeting worshipers after the Sunday morning service, Anne stands next to him with a cassette recorder in her purse. She asks the name of each visiting woman. If the woman doesn't pronounce her name clearly, Anne will ask her to repeat it or spell it—so the recorder is sure to pick it up.

The next day she goes to the church office to look for the visitor cards of those whose names her cassette player has recorded. Then she calls each woman and makes an appointment to visit her with an EE team. Often when she leads such a person to Christ she will invite her and her husband to dinner at the manse. This gives Dr. Kennedy an opportunity to lead the husband to the Lord. Jim Kennedy once told me that Anne, by simply obeying Christ's command to witness, may have led more people to the Lord than anyone else in their evangelism ministry. What a beautiful example of teamwork!

Changing the metaphor from fishing to farming, Paul speaks of similar teamwork: "I planted the seed, Apollos watered it, but God made it grow" (1 Corinthians 3:6).

How can you involve other believers in bringing your non-Christian friends to Christ? By asking them to pray for the salvation of your unsaved friends. By asking them to join you for dinner—or a sporting event or a fun activity—with a friend who does not know Christ.

In the context of such Christian fellowship your non-Christian friends will experience a depth of reality, truth and love that the world does not and cannot offer. This kind of experience will cause them to ask, "What is it that makes such a difference?"

Observe also that such . . .

c. Interdependence maximizes the use of our various gifts and skills.

In recent years there has been much biblical teaching on the gifts of the Spirit. Probably you have been taught that each believer has at least one gift and that no believer has all the gifts. Therefore we should utilize the gifts that we have to edify one another within the Body of Christ—that is, the church. That is all very true. But not enough is being said about using those gifts outside the body to win the lost! We must also use those God-given gifts, together with our natural talents and learned skills, to reach nonbelievers!

You may, for example, have the gift of hospitality, but not of teaching. Why not work together with a fellow believer who is gifted in teaching and organize an evangelistic home Bible study? You could provide the home and the refreshments while he or she leads the study. With a little creativity you can involve your fellow believers and help them utilize their gifts in reaching the lost.

A Christian medical doctor in Sioux City, Iowa, contracted the construction of his vacation home to a builder in Omaha. The doctor developed a warm friendship with the man, reaching out to him many times with the love of Christ. But somehow he wasn't able to win him to Christ.

Then one day the builder was found to be full of cancer and not expected to live but a few weeks. His doctor friend in Sioux City grew more concerned than ever for the salvation of the man, but he didn't know what to do. Someone told him about Christ Community Church and the friendship evangelists whom we have equipped through EE. One day when I was out of the office he called, leaving the name, address and phone number of his builder friend. He described his physical condition and asked if I could send "one of your team" to call on him.

Annie, whom I've mentioned before, is not only well-trained in EE, but she also has a gift of mercy. She loves to visit the sick and minister to hurting people. She is especially effective with people who are near the end of life. She is so compassionate, thoughtful and gracious that no one can reject her ministry and witness.

Annie and her sister went to visit the builder and his wife. On their first visit they mentioned that the doctor in Sioux City was concerned about the couple and asked them to visit. On that visit they sought just to become acquainted and build a friendship. In fact, they made several more visits to deepen the relationship, reaching out to the couple in practical ways.   Finally, when Annie sensed the builder was ready, she asked for permission to share her testimony and the gospel. The wife left the bedroom while Annie talked to her husband. Before the visit ended he prayed to invite Christ into his life.

As Annie left the room, she found the wife just outside the door crying. "Can I help you in some way?" Annie inquired. The builder's wife assured Annie her tears were tears of joy. She said she had been listening and had prayed along with her husband to receive Christ!

The builder is now in heaven. His wife is enjoying abundant, eternal life here on earth! And the Christian doctor in Sioux City is praising God for fellow believers who were equipped, available and gifted to help him reach his friend for Christ.

As you involve fellow believers in reaching your non-Christian friends, you will be amazed how each of you complements the other and contributes toward a loving, balanced, effective witness.

Jesus' second important lesson about evangelism bears the surprising heading:

2. Failing

> "I'm going out to fish," Simon Peter told them, and they said, "We'll go with you." So they went out and got into the boat, but that night they caught nothing.
>
> Early in the morning, Jesus stood on the shore, but the disciples did not realize that it was Jesus.
>
> He called out to them, "Friends, haven't you any fish?"
>
> "No," they answered. (John 21:3-5)

Some of the best lessons in life are learned from our failures and mistakes. The disciples had learned many lessons during their three years with Jesus, but their Master Teacher had one more important principle to communicate. It was that . . .

a. Self-sufficiency ultimately leads to failure.

Notice with what confidence Peter announces, "I'm going out to fish." Failure was not in the minds of any of the seven as they boarded the boat. But note the result of their toil: "That night they caught nothing." *Nothing!* A whole long night of work and nothing to show for it.

Jesus (whom at first they do not recognize) only adds to their embarrassment by appearing on the scene and asking, "Friends, haven't you any fish?"

In the every day pursuits of life, it often pays to increase your efforts. To try a little harder. To work a little longer. To exercise a little more willpower. To believe in yourself a little more firmly. Then you'll accomplish what you set out to do. Then you'll be successful. Such human strategies may sometimes work in the secular realm. I say "sometimes," because it didn't seem to produce any results for Peter and his fishing team!

I'm sure God intervened to keep the fish away from the nets that night, because He wanted to teach "Peter & company" a lesson. He wanted Peter and the other disciples to know that maximum self effort isn't always enough.

Raymond shared the gospel with a young woman, Mary. Initially she said she wanted to receive Christ. But then Raymond offered her a spiritual birth certificate and began to explain what was involved in her decision. At that point she changed her mind and said she wasn't ready for such a commitment. Raymond was downcast. He had failed. He wondered what he had done wrong.

Five years later Raymond and his wife were at a supermarket. As they reached the checkout counter, they discovered that their friend Mary was working there as a cashier! Mary said she wanted to touch base with the couple. She asked if she might call them.

When Mary called, Raymond and his wife arranged a meeting. They learned from Mary that five years earlier she had "been on drugs and alcohol and was using foul language." Now she was ready to turn her life over to God and to trust Him to help her live by the commitment set forth on the spiritual birth certificate. Since then God has completely changed her life. She has led her husband to Christ and last Christmas she was, of all things, an angel in her church's Christmas pageant!

True, your efforts sometimes may fail. Perhaps it is not yet God's time. Perhaps the "fruit is not yet ripe." You need always to remember that . . .

**b. Christ wants us to see that without Him
we can do nothing of eternal value.**

The psalmist spoke about this: "It is better to
take refuge in the LORD than to trust in princes"
(Psalm 118:9). And Jeremiah adds, "Cursed is
the one who trusts in man, who depends on
flesh for his strength. . . . But blessed is the man
who trusts in the LORD, whose confidence is in
him" (Jeremiah 17:5-7). Jesus stated it in even
more unmistakable terms: "I am the vine; you
are the branches. If a man remains in me and I
in him, he will bear much fruit; apart from me
you can do nothing" (John 15:5).

The disciples were about to have a clear
demonstration of this truth in their familiar occupation of . . .

3. Fishing

> [Jesus] said, "Throw your net on the
> right side of the boat and you will find
> some [fish]." When they did, they
> were unable to haul the net in because
> of the large number of fish.
>
> Then the disciple whom Jesus loved
> said to Peter, "It is the Lord!" As soon
> as Simon Peter heard him say, "It is
> the Lord," he wrapped his outer gar-
> ment around him (for he had taken it
> off) and jumped into the water. The
> other disciples followed in the boat,

towing the net full of fish, for they were not far from shore, about a hundred yards. When they landed, they saw a fire of burning coals there with fish on it, and some bread.

Jesus said to them, "Bring some of the fish you have just caught."

Simon Peter climbed aboard and dragged the net ashore. It was full of large fish, 153, but even with so many the net was not torn. (21:6-11)

a. Christ is the One who controls responsiveness.

When this unidentified Stranger on the shore told the seven disciples to throw their net on the right side of the boat, He was in fact demonstrating unforgettably to them that He needed to be in control of their lives. He who knew where the fish were in the Sea of Galilee would know where the responsive people were when these disciples became true "fishers of men" (see Matthew 4:19). If they would trust and obey Him, they would be unusually successful in their fishing.

b. Christ's way produces abundant results.

It was something of a miracle that these seasoned fishermen would accept orders from a Stranger on shore. But when they did and cast their net where He told them to, "they were unable to haul the net in because of the large number of fish" (21:6). Seeing such amazing results, John recognized the Stranger Who had produced such amazing results. "It is the Lord!" he said to Peter.

In the spiritual realm as well as the temporal, only God can produce abundant, abiding results. Both the Old Testament and the New support that statement.

> Unless the LORD builds the house,
>   its builders labor in vain.
> Unless the LORD watches over the city,
>   the watchmen stand guard in vain.
>   (Psalm 127:1)

> Neither he who plants nor he who waters is anything, but only God, who makes things grow. (1 Corinthians 3:7)

Your methods, strategies, schemes and plans will avail nothing without Christ's divine intervention. Your evangelistic endeavors and your trust must be in Him, for He alone can bring conviction of sin. He alone can open people's blind eyes to see the truth. He alone can melt their stony hearts. He alone can bring about the miracle of new birth.

The sooner you recognize, as John did, that "It is the Lord!" the sooner you will begin to do evangelism the Lord's way. And the sooner you will see results similarly marked by increased numbers.

A few years ago I was invited to teach an EE

Leadership Training Clinic for 25 Vietnamese pastors and lay leaders at Santa Ana, California. The five-day clinic was to be followed by three evenings of evangelistic meetings in a local high school auditorium, where I was to be the speaker. I prepared and prayed much for the ministry, but on the flight from Omaha to California I had misgivings.

It's been 15 years, I thought to myself, *since the fall of Vietnam. The Vietnamese in Santa Ana are no longer refugees. They are comfortably situated with well-paying jobs, homes of their own and nice cars. I doubt that they feel any need for God. I'm sure they won't be interested in the gospel. Why did I accept this invitation to spend a whole week among unresponsive people? I'm wasting my time!*

God has since forgiven me for my pessimism. As I taught in the EE clinic and went out with teams into the homes of the people's Vietnamese friends, relatives and neighbors, I saw how well the church had prepared for that week. People responded to the gospel with an openness I have seldom seen. On each night of the evangelistic campaign, the auditorium was packed with more unbelieving friends and relatives. The people trained in the clinic served as counselors. During the week over 200 people responded to Christ! The results were far beyond my wildest dreams. And I gave—and give—Jesus Christ all the praise and glory, for He did it!

But you ask, "Should we really be so con-

cerned about large numbers of people coming
to Christ? Is quantity important?" To those
questions I respond with a very positive "Yes!"
And I base it largely on the fact that . . .

c. Christ is concerned about numbers.

The seven disciples had great difficulty haul-
ing in the net "because of the large number of
fish" (21:6). A little later Peter took time to actually count the catch: 153 "large fish" (21:11).

There are well-meaning Christians who try to
convince us that God isn't concerned about
numbers. He's not interested in quantity, only
quality. The truth is, if you examine the holy
Scriptures carefully, you will see that He is concerned about both. In this instance, God has
seen fit to include both the quantity of fish
(153) and their quality (large).

In Acts, Luke describes the early church in
both terms. First he offers a qualitative assessment: "The church throughout Judea, Galilee
and Samaria enjoyed a time of peace. It was
strengthened." Then Luke adds a quantitative
assessment: "encouraged by the Holy Spirit, it
grew in numbers"(9:31).

It's probably safe to say that you can't have
one without the other. In the work of Christ
you must aim for both quantity and quality.

Tom's dad, who had Alzheimer's, finally
died at age 88. But not before Tom had a
chance to lead him to Christ. Two months
before his death, Tom's dad had a period of

very normal consciousness during which Tom had opportunity to carefully, clearly set forth the gospel.

At the funeral Tom told his brother, Dave, that their dad had made a decision to trust Christ and was now in heaven. A few days later, Tom got a call on his car phone. It was Dave, who wanted to know how he could be saved. It was late in the afternoon, so Tom presented the gospel to Dave over the car phone—exactly what he had shared with their dad. And to his great delight Dave invited Christ into his life!

When Tom got home he told his wife, Denise, the news. She could hardly believe it! But before long Dave showed up at their front door and confirmed Tom's words. He had come, he said, out of concern for his wife, Marcia. She wasn't saved.

Tom suggested that he and Denise could go over to their home that evening and share the gospel with Marcia. But Dave insisted that he should do it himself—if only he could get some pointers from Tom and Denise. So Tom gave Dave a "Do You Know for Sure?" booklet and walked him through the steps, the prayer and the "new birth certificate."

When Dave reached home, booklet in hand, Marcia told him she had just been listening to Charles Stanley over the air. She was ready to trust Christ. Add one more to the kingdom!

But that is not the end of the story. Marcia

called Tom and Denise to tell them she was
trusting Christ as her Savior and Lord. But she
was concerned about some of her family and
her neighbors. If she invited a few of them to a
potluck dinner, would Tom and Denise be willing to share the gospel?

At the appointed time Tom and Denise were
there. Marcia had invited 15 people in all—her
mother and father, her two sons and one
daughter by a previous marriage, her sister and
nine other relatives and friends.

"I invited you," Marcia announced, "so you
could hear what Tom and Denise shared with
Dave and me." At the end of the evening three of
the 15 prayed to receive Christ. Since then, one-
by-one, the others are gradually turning to Christ!

Is God concerned about numbers? Ask rather,
"Is God concerned about *all* of His perishing
creation?" The Bible is clear: "God so loved the
world" (John 3:16). That excludes none of the
nearly 6 billion people on our planet.

4. Feeding

> Jesus said to them, "Come and have
> breakfast." None of the disciples
> dared ask him, "Who are you?" They
> knew it was the Lord. Jesus came,
> took the bread and gave it to them,
> and did the same with the fish. This
> was now the third time Jesus ap-
> peared to his disciples after he was

raised from the dead.

When they had finished eating, Jesus said to Simon Peter, "Simon son of John, do you truly love me more than these?"

"Yes, Lord," he said, "you know that I love you."

Jesus said, "Feed my lambs."

Again Jesus said, "Simon son of John, do you truly love me?"

He answered, "Yes, Lord, you know that I love you."

Jesus answered, "Take care of my sheep."

The third time he said to him, "Simon son of John, do you love me?"

Peter was hurt because Jesus asked him the third time, "Do you love me?" He said, "Lord, you know all things; you know that I love you."

Jesus said, "Feed my sheep." (21:12-17)

a. "Feeding" must follow "fishing."

In this historical narrative, Christ moves from fishing to feeding: "Jesus said to them, 'Come and have breakfast' "(21:12) and "Feed my lambs" (21:15). Having offered Peter a lesson in fishing for men—evangelism—Jesus now turns to a lesson on feeding lambs—the follow-up of new believers. It is crucial that you give adequate attention to the follow-up and spiritual feeding of the people whom God allows you to lead to Christ.

b. *Agape* **(divine) love in essential to effective follow-up.**

How interesting that each of the three times in which Jesus charges Peter to feed/tend His lambs/sheep, He asks Peter about his love. Caring for new believers is hard work. It requires the expenditure of much time. Only love for Christ and the love that Christ gives will enable you to give proper attention to the new believers for whom you are responsible.

c. New believers, like lambs, need much tender care.

W. Phillip Keller in his book, *A Shepherd Looks at Psalm 23*, observes that, of all domestic animals, sheep require the most care. It is interesting that here Christ likens new believers to lambs.

It is not enough for you to give new believers follow-up booklets, Gospels of John, Bible lessons and tapes. You must bring them into your personal life, share meals together, pray with them, help them through difficult times of testing and temptation and generally be to them a spiritual parent until such time as they can stand on their own feet, feed themselves and begin reproducing Christ in the lives of others.

Several years ago Joe and Nancy moved to

Omaha. They bought a home across the circle from Tom and Denise. Joe, age 34, found a position at a large computer company. Nancy was a homemaker caring for five-year-old Joey. As the two couples worked around their homes, gardening and mowing their lawns, they began to build a warm friendship. In conversation the two men discovered they both came from the same religious background. Since Tom had subsequently turned his life over to Jesus Christ, he had a natural opportunity to explain briefly why he was no longer a part of that former religion. Tom wanted to go into more detail, but he sensed Joe's edginess, so he backed off and changed the subject.

For five years Tom didn't raise the matter again. Meanwhile, Joe and Nancy were having marital problems. In fact, the whole neighborhood became aware of their disagreements. Unbeknown to Tom, Joe and Nancy began going from church to church searching for the message Tom had offered to share with them, hoping it might resolve their marital conflicts. They were too embarrassed to ask Tom, afraid he would look down on them.

But one Sunday night as Tom was returning home from church, Bible in his hand, Joe shouted across the street to him, "Tom, what's on your schedule? Can you come over here and tell us again how we can have eternal life?" Half the neighborhood could hear Joe as he yelled out his invitation!

That night Tom shared with two very eager people the difference between religion and a relationship with Christ. Joe and Nancy both prayed to receive Christ.

As they were saying goodnight to Tom, they told him how they had watched him and Denise and just knew by their lives that what Tom had started to share five years earlier had to be the truth. "We only regret we've waited so long to get back to you," they added.

That's the discipling process that Christ modeled and mandated for all of His followers! And this thought leads me to the last point suggested by this concluding chapter of John's gospel:

5. Following

> Jesus said [to Peter], . . . "I tell you the truth, when you were younger you dressed yourself and went where you wanted; but when you are old you will stretch out your hands, and someone else will dress you and lead you where you do not want to go." Jesus said this to indicate the kind of death by which Peter would glorify God. Then he said to him, "Follow me!"
>
> Peter turned and saw that the disciple whom Jesus loved was following

them. (This was the one who had leaned back against Jesus at supper and had said, "Lord, who is going to betray you?") When Peter saw him, he asked, "Lord, what about him?"

Jesus answered, "If I want him to remain alive until I return, what is that to you? You must follow me." (21:17-22)

In the closing verses of John 21, Jesus twice commands Peter, "Follow me!" Each seems to have a somewhat different focus.

a. Following Christ always involves a cross.

Jesus hints to Peter that his life will end in martyrdom upon a cross. Earlier Jesus had said to Peter and all His disciples, "If anyone would come after me, he must deny himself and take up his cross and follow me" (Matthew 16:24).

It's the same today. If you are going to follow Christ fishing for men and feeding His lambs, you will have to deny yourselves and take up your cross. Such a life involves sacrifice and death to self, but it also leads to fruitfulness and fulfilled living!

b. Following Christ means focusing on Him, not others.

When Christ unveiled to Peter the culmination of his life in martyrdom, Peter quickly pointed to John and asked, "Lord, what about him?" But Jesus gently rebuked Peter saying, "If I want him to remain alive until I return, what is that to you? You must follow me."

In your life and service for Christ, it is easy to shift your eyes from Christ to your fellow workers. That can be harmful. To be happy, content, properly directed and fruitful, you must ever keep your eyes upon the Blessed One you are following: Christ! He will never disappoint or mislead you! His smile of approval will be your best reward!

Dave and Pattie have two children, Jessica and Josh. Dave and Pattie were concerned that their children come to know Christ at an early age and enthrone Him as Lord. So friendship evangelism for them started at home with their family.

Would you believe that at age two Jessica started thinking about this important matter? One night she climbed into bed with her daddy and said, "Ask Jesus into my heart—go to heaven some day."

Dave didn't understand what she meant and replied, "Yes, Honey, that's great!"

Three times she repeated the same statement without her dad's realizing what she was driving at. Finally she insisted emphatically, "No, Daddy. Ask Jesus into my heart *now*—go to heaven some day!" Dave realized Jessica wanted to receive Christ right then. He sat up in bed and explained the gospel in terms a child could understand. Then he led Jessica in a simple prayer to invite Jesus into her life.

A few years later, when her brother Josh was two and a half, Jessica and Josh climbed into bed with their father, and Jessica said to Josh, "When Jesus comes, Mommy and Daddy and Jessica are going to heaven." Afraid he'd get left behind, little Josh grabbed his daddy's pajama shirt tails and "hung on for dear life!"

Jessica proceeded thereafter to remind her little brother that he needed to ask Jesus into his heart. And one happy day Dave had the joy of leading his son to faith in Christ.

But as their children grew older, Dave and Pattie became concerned that the two children wouldn't understand or remember the commitments they had made at such an early age. Then a friend, Mel, suggested to them something that really made sense. He explained that children come to an age somewhere between eight and 12 when they move from taking things by simple faith to reasoning things through. So when it becomes evident a child is entering into the reasoning mode, the parent needs to find an opportune time to talk to the child and help him or her reason through the earlier act of faith.

So the day came for Jessica, and later for Josh, when Dave and Pattie sat them down and explained, "You're coming to a new stage in your life when you need to reason through what you do. When you were two years old, you asked Jesus into your heart. Did you really mean that? Are you going to go on with that decision? Okay, let's pray and tell Jesus you remember that time, and you want to continue trusting Him as long as you live."

That experience became for the two children a confirmation of what they had done. It gave them a strong foundation to build on.

When Jessica became a teenager she signed up for an eight-week short-term missions trip to Europe. While in the two-week "boot camp" and then during the six weeks in Europe she heard people talking about biblical truths and principles which her mom and dad had taught her. She thought to herself, "Maybe Mom and Dad are on to something!" This helped her to "internalize" the Lordship issue. And the beliefs she had earlier held now became deeply rooted convictions she could stand and grow on.

Entering her junior year of high school, Jessica found herself in a class entitled "The Bible as Mythology." She started standing up for what she believed, but few of the other Christians in class spoke out with her for the truth. Having had EE training in her youth group, she was firm in her convictions. She also asked her dad for his college notes that dealt with the truth of the Scriptures. She made copies of these and distributed them to her Christian classmates to help them also refute the teacher's erroneous material.

When asked how she could be so bold, Jessica replied, "I can challenge this heretical teaching because I have my own values, not just my parents'." Being so well equipped, she reached out in friendship evangelism to three of her school friends: Jill while on campus, Sarah while riding with her dad to a nearby city, and Jenny while "goofing around" at the church.

✻ ✻ ✻

Friendship evangelism. For three years I have made a concentrated study of the Scriptures with one major question in mind: How did Jesus and the early Christians evangelize their friends and neighbors? What was their method of evangelism?

I am overwhelmingly convinced that the gospel spreads most effectively across an existing network of trust relationships: friends, relatives, associates, neighbors. It was true in Bible times, as I have showed you. It is true today, as many of the illustrations in this book testify. Because the gospel travels best through established relationships, you and I certainly should be using those channels and cultivating those relationships.

If Jesus had a "mission statement," it was this: "The Son of Man came to seek and to save what was lost" (Luke 19:10). And He has given a rather similar one to His disciples: "As the Father has sent me, I am sending you" (John 20:21). (You *do* classify yourself as one of His disciples, don't you?)

Jesus Himself had more than one method of

evangelism: For example, He preached. He also taught. But He often evangelized person-to-person, friend-to-friend. Friendship evangelism is probably the most natural, least threatening way that you can evangelize. Couple that fact with the fact that many people are secretly searching for a satisfying meaning to life, and you have a win-win situation.

Well, nearly. It is win-win if your witness is consistent—if your life and lips express the same message. What about preparation? Have you prepared yourself to witness effectively? Have you been formally trained through EE or some other evangelism course? What about prayer? Prayer is the *sine qua non* of all spiritual endeavor. Are you praying for your friends, relatives, associates and neighbors? Are you alert to the opportunities God opens up to you?

Christ set forth the right way to evangelize lost people. I encourage you to apply His first century principles to your 21st century relationships. They will not fail!

Discussion Questions

1. What was Jesus' way of evangelism? Why do you think it might be good to follow His example today even though we are living and evangelizing centuries later?

2. From the Scriptures that were the

basis of our study in this chapter, how do you see fellowship and friendship evangelism interrelated and mutually supportive?

3. Why is teamwork important in friendship evangelism? How do spiritual gifts enter into friendship evangelism?

4. What possible good can come from failures in friendship evangelism? Why do you think just trying a little harder or doing it a little smarter is not the answer when you fail?

5. Ultimately, who controls the responsiveness of the people you seek to bring to Christ? Why is that important to understand? Since it is true, what might you endeavor to do?

6. Do you think keeping statistics has any place in evangelism? Explain.

7. Why is *agape* love essential to effective follow-up?

8. What is meant by the expression, "crucified with Christ"? Why is crucifixion necessary? What might it mean in your life as you try to win people to Christ through friendship?

Do You Know
for Sure?

DO YOU KNOW FOR SURE that you are going to be with God in heaven? If God were to ask you, "Why should I let you into my heaven?" what would you say?

If you are uncertain or hesitant—even for a moment—to answer that question, you are about to read the best news you could ever hear! The few minutes it will take you to read these pages may be the most important time you will ever spend!

Did you know the Bible tells how you can know for sure that you have eternal life and will go to be with God in heaven? "I write these things to you . . . so that you may know that you have eternal life" (1 John 5:13).

Here is how you can know for sure.

1. *Heaven (eternal life) is a free gift.* The Bible says, "The gift of God is eternal life in Christ Jesus our Lord" (Romans 6:23).

And because heaven is a gift like any other genuine gift, *it is not earned or deserved*. Therefore, no amount of personal effort, good works or religious deeds can earn a place in heaven for you. "By grace you have been saved, through faith—and this not from yourselves, it is the gift of God—not by works, so that no one can boast" (Ephesians 2:8–9).

Why can you not earn your way to heaven? Because . . .

2. *Like everyone else, you are a sinner.* The Bible declares, "All have sinned and fall short of the glory of God" (Romans 3:23).

Sin is transgressing God's law and includes such things as lying, lust, cheating, deceit, anger, evil thoughts, immoral behavior and more. And because of transgressions like these, *you cannot save yourself.*

If you wanted to save yourself by good deeds, do you know how good you would have to be? The Bible says you would have to be *perfect.* "Be perfect, therefore, as your heavenly Father is perfect" (Matthew 5:48).

With such a high standard, you cannot save yourself, for God also says, "Whoever keeps the whole law and yet stumbles at just one point is guilty of breaking all of it" (James 2:10).

In spite of your sin, however . . .

3. *God is merciful. He does not want to punish you.* This is because "God is love" (1 John 4:8) and He says, "I have loved you with an everlasting love" (Jeremiah 31:3).

But the same Bible that tells us that God loves us also tells us that *God is just, and therefore He must punish sin.* He says, "He does not leave the guilty unpunished" (Exodus 34:7) and "The soul who sins is the one who will die" (Ezekiel 18:4).

We have a problem: We have all sinned. The penalty for sin is death. We need forgiveness so that we can have a right relationship with God. *God solved this problem for us in the Person of . . .*

4. *Jesus Christ the Lord.* Exactly who would you say Jesus Christ is? The Bible tells us clearly that He is the infinite God-Man: "In the beginning was the Word [Jesus], and the Word [Jesus] was with God, and the Word [Jesus] was God. . . . The Word [Jesus] became flesh and made his dwelling among us" (John 1:1, 14).

Jesus Christ came to earth and lived a sinless life. But while He was on earth, *what did He do?* He died on the cross to pay the penalty for your sins and rose from the grave to purchase a place for you in heaven. "We all, like sheep, have gone astray, each of us has turned to his own way; and the LORD has laid on him [Jesus] the iniquity of us all" (Isaiah 53:6).

God hates your sins. Because of His love for you, He has placed those sins on His Son. Christ Jesus bore your sin in His body on the cross. Therefore He is offering you eternal life—heaven—as a free gift!

This gift is received by . . .

5. *Faith.* Faith is the key that will open the door to heaven for you. Many people mistake two things for saving faith:

a. Mere *intellectual assent*, that is, believing certain historical facts. The Bible says the devil believes in God, so believing in God is not saving faith.

b. Mere *temporal faith*, that is, trusting God for temporary crises such as financial, family or physical needs. It is good for you to trust Christ for these things, but this is not saving faith.

Saving faith is trusting in Jesus Christ alone for salvation. It means resting upon Christ alone and what He has done rather than upon what you have done to get yourself into heaven. "Believe [trust] in the Lord Jesus, and you will be saved" (Acts 16:31).

Faith is like the hand of a beggar receiving the gift of a king. We do not deserve the gift of eternal life. But we can have it if we will receive it by faith.

You have just read the greatest story ever told about the greatest offer ever made by the greatest Person who ever lived—Jesus Christ the Lord. The question that God is asking you now is, *Would you like to receive the gift of eternal life?*

Because this is such an important matter, let us clarify what it involves.

a. It means, first, that you *transfer your trust*

from what you have been doing to what Christ has done for you on the cross.

b. It means, next, that you *receive the resurrected, living Christ into your life as Savior.* Jesus says, "Here I am! I stand at the door [of your life] and knock. If anyone hears my voice and opens the door, I will come in" (Revelation 3:20).

c. It means further that you *receive Jesus Christ into your life as Lord.* He comes as Master and King. There is a throne room in your heart, and that throne rightly belongs to Jesus. He made you. He bought you and He wants to take His rightful place on the throne of your life.

d. It means, finally, that you *repent of your sins.* By that you turn from anything you have been doing that is not pleasing to God and you follow Him as He reveals His will to you in His Word.

6. *Prayer.* Now, if you really want eternal life, *you can pray to God right where you are.* Right now you can receive His gift of eternal life through Jesus Christ.

"It is with your heart that you believe and are justified, and it is with your mouth that you confess and are saved. . . . 'Everyone who calls on the name of the Lord will be saved' " (Romans 10:10, 13).

If you want to receive the gift of eternal life through Jesus Christ, then call on Him, asking Him for this gift right now.

Here is a suggested prayer:

Lord Jesus Christ, I know I am a sinner and do not deserve eternal life. But I believe You died and rose from the grave to purchase a place in heaven for me. Lord Jesus, come into my life; take control of my life; forgive my sins and save me. I repent of my sins and now place my trust in You for my salvation. I accept Your free gift of eternal life. Amen.

If that prayer is the desire of your heart, look at what Jesus promises to those who believe in Him: "I tell you the truth, he who believes has everlasting life" (John 6:47).

7. *Welcome to God's family!* If you have truly repented of (forsaken, turned away from) your sins, placed your trust in Jesus Christ's sacrificial death and received the gift of eternal life, you are now a child of God! Forever! Welcome to the family!

"To all who received him, to those who believed in his name, he gave the right to become children of God" (John 1:12).

8. *Today is your spiritual birthday*—a day you will want to remember always! "Born not of natural descent, nor of human decision or a husband's will, but born of God" (John 1:13).

When you were physically born, the day of your birth was attested by a birth certificate. And so, today, to help you recall what God has done in your life on this important day, we invite you to sign and keep the *Spiritual Birth Certificate :*

SPIRITUAL BIRTH CERTIFICATE

"Everyone who calls on the name of the Lord will be saved" (Romans 10:13).

Knowing that I have sinned and that I need the Lord Jesus Christ as my Savior, I now turn from my sins and trust Jesus for my eternal life. I ask Jesus Christ to forgive me and to deliver me from sin's power and to give me eternal life.

I now give Jesus Christ control of my life.

From this time forward, as God gives me strength, I will seek to serve Him and obey Him in all areas of my life.

Signature _____
Date _____

---

9. *What is next?* Just as a newborn baby grows physically, so you will grow spiritually by taking the following steps:

a. Read one chapter of the book of John (in the Bible) each day. "Like newborn babies, crave pure spiritual milk, so that by it you may grow up in your salvation" (1 Peter 2:2).

b. Spend time each day in prayer, conversing with God. "Do not be anxious about anything, but in everything, by prayer and petition, with thanksgiving, present your requests to God" (Philippians 4:6).

c. Worship regularly in a church that teaches you the Bible and honors Jesus Christ. "I rejoice with those who said to me, 'Let us go to the house of the LORD' " (Psalm 122:1).

"God is Spirit, and his worshipers must worship in spirit and in truth" (John 4:24).

"Let us not give up meeting together, as some are in the habit of doing" (Hebrews 10:25).

d. Fellowship with Christians who will help you grow in faith. "Those who accepted [Peter's] message . . . devoted themselves to the apostles' teaching and to the fellowship, to the breaking of bread and to prayer" (Acts 2:41–42).

e. Be a witness by telling others what Jesus Christ means to you.

Jesus said, "Whoever acknowledges me before men, I will also acknowledge him before my Father in heaven. But whoever disowns me before men, I will disown him before my Father in heaven" (Matthew 10:32–33).

Six- Step Approach
to
Friendship Evangelism

The diagram on the next page is a tool to be used in charting your friendship evangelism approach over a one-year period. It can, of course, be shortened or lengthened as the need arises. I suggest that you use one page per person—a friend, relative, associate or neighbor—and write his or her name in the blank above.

Try to complete one step every two months. The first column lists the goal for each step and the second column gives two suggestions for some things you may want to do or some places you may want to go to attempt your goal. If these suggestions don't fit your situation, then choose something that will fit both yours and your friend's schedules and preferences.

Six-Step Approach to Friendship Evangelism

His or Her Name: _____

STEP	ACTION
1	**Date____**
Develop Personal Acquantaince	*Talk over the fence or have coffee together*
2	**Date____**
Use secular life for further involvement	*Go to a ball game or shop together*
3	**Date____**
Share and observe family values	*Have lunch or a barbecue at your home*
4	**Date____**
Discuss church background	*Relax together at a picnic or fishing trip*
5	**Date____**
Give your personal testimony	*Meet for golfing or sewing*
6	**Date____**
Share the gospel	*Invite him or her to a church or to dinner*